M000266328

ERITREA:
REVOLUTION AT DUSK

Photographs and Text by
ROBERT PAPSTEIN

THE RED SEA PRESS
Publishers & Distributors of Third World Books
15 Industry Court
Trenton, NJ 08638
(609) 771-1666

Eritrea Basic Facts

Population: 3.5 million—60 U.N. members have less population.

Ethnic composition: Nine nationalities.

Religion: Highlands—Coptic Christian; Lowlands—Nomadic Muslim.

Surface: 124,320 sq. km. (47,754 sq. mi.), about the size of England or Austria; 62 U.N. member states are smaller.

Ports: Massawa and Asab on the Red Sea.

Cultivable land: 6,500,000 acres

Pasture: 22,997,000

Commercially exploitable mineral reserves: iron, copper, gold, potash, and potentially petroleum and natural gas.

Major urban areas: Asmara, Massawa

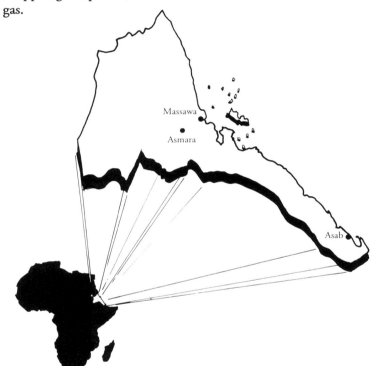

The Red Sea Press, Inc.
15 Industry Court
Trenton, New Jersey 08638

First Printing 1991

Book design by Robert Papstein
Typesetting by Malcolm Litchfield · This book is composed in Adobe Garamond

Library of Congress Catalog Card Number: 90-81661

| 0-932415-63-6 | Cloth |
| 0-932415-64-4 | Paper |

Dedicated To Those Who Are Creating Eritrea

PREFACE

On May 25th, 1991, after thirty years of military struggle, the fighters of the Eritrean People's Liberation Front (EPLF) smashed through the lines of a demoralized Ethiopian army and occupied the Eritrean capital of Asmara, bringing to an end a generation of Ethiopian colonialism and Africa's longest and most costly war.

Five years ago, when this book was started, famine and war raged in Eritrea and even though the EPLF's military successes were already remarkable, I always left Eritrea with a mixture of optimism and sadness. Optimism because of the indomitable Eritrean will to achieve their independence; sadness because, alone, they faced a massive Ethiopian army supported by the superpower military resources of the Soviet Union.

We always said goodbye in the same way; surely next year we would sit in a cafe along one of Asmara's tree lined streets sipping ginger-laced coffee, thankful that the war was over. No matter how much we might have dreamed about it, even with increasing EPLF military successes, after more than a quarter century of war, peace still seemed remote.

Each time I visited Eritrea the improvements were remarkable; a clear demonstration that the EPLF's commitment to self-reliant development was working—even in the midst of war and famine. Small, underground EPLF workshops were able to rebuild captured weapons to sustain the military struggle; a largely illiterate population was learning to read; primary medical services were expanding; the underground pharmacy was coming ever closer to producing sufficient basic medicines to meet local needs while the commitment to social change had engendered a debate and created institutions which were transforming every level of Eritrean society.

Everyone who was following politics in the Horn of Africa knew that Ethiopia was disintegrating internally. The Dergue, the government controlled by President Mengistu Haile Mariam, was unwilling to address any of the internal political problems which had plagued Ethiopia for a century and was squandering the resources of a desperately poor country by fighting not only the EPLF, which wanted independence for the former Italian colony of Eritrea (which Ethiopia had annexed in 1962), but also the Tigray People's Liberation Front (TPLF) and other revolutionary groups who were seeking to create representative political institutions within a restructured, federal Ethiopia.

Changes in the Soviet Union, eastern Europe (once a major supporter of Mengistu) and especially the increasing efficiency of the EPLF, TPLF and others, together with Mengistu's regular, demoralizing purges of the army and civil service created a growing awareness among Ethiopian opinion makers that they were fighting hopeless wars. With the newly formed Ethiopian People's Revolutionary Democratic Movement marching on Addis Abba, the capital, and with ninety percent of Eritrea in the hands of the EPLF, Mengistu fled the country, abandoning his armies in the field and his closest advisors in the government.

In June the EPLF declared a provisional government in Eritrea and asked the United Nations to take up the responsibility it has shirked for thirty years, to supervise free elections. After a generation of struggle, Eritrean independence, with all of the difficulties and complications which will follow, now seems assured.

During the struggle against Ethiopian colonialism the EPLF developed a unique policy of self-reliant development which, in spite of war, chronic drought and catastrophic famine, has created an infrastructure in Eritrea which would be the envy of many developing countries in the region. The Eritrean story is therefore not only one of delayed political justice, it also offers insights into new approaches to economic planning at a time when Africa is desperately in need of alternatives to the type of "development" which, after a generation, has resulted in debt and impoverishment.

CONTENTS

Introduction   1

    Historical Background   3

Traditions: Nomads and Farmers   11

Challenge   25

    Politics of Independence   27

    The War for Independence   35

    The Price   61

    Famine   77

    Refugees   87

    Orphans 105

Transformations 113

    Women 115

    Education 137

    Health 147

Bibliography 168

Further Information 169

The social change brought about through military struggle and education are creating modern Eritrea. Near Janni adults hang their captured AK-47 assault rifles on tree branches while learning basic mathematics.

INTRODUCTION

In 1962, Haile Selassie, Emperor of Ethiopia and the representative of Western interests in the Horn of Africa, annexed the former Italian colony of Eritrea which Ethiopia had administered under United Nations auspices for a decade. The world turned away from Eritrean cries of injustice; the independence of Eritrea was sacrificed to the imperial ambitions of Ethiopia and the geopolitical concerns of the Cold War. After years of unsuccessful pleading to the United Nations and to the world at large, a few Eritreans managed to steal two pistols and attacked an Ethiopian police station. That was 30 years ago—the beginning of Africa's longest war and most remarkable social revolution.

No one in Eritrea under the age of 30 knows life without war. With a population of 3.5 million, alone, without allies, without military support from the outside, Eritreans are systematically defeating Africa's third largest army (recruited from a country with 42 million people), supported for a decade by the full force of the Soviet Union. Soviet supplied Migs, bombs and napalm have forced Eritreans to live and work underground in bunkers. The revolution renews itself each day at dusk, when the coming darkness makes it too dangerous for the Migs to fly; food relief convoys start their first-gear crawl through the mountains, military units shift positions, farmers plough their fields and a hundred little workshops start their generators to produce the necessities of survival. The Eritrean People's Liberation Front (EPLF) has evolved into what one intelligence source describes as "the most effective guerrilla army in the world."

Eritreans have survived a generation of war and years of chronic hunger. Eritrea was at the center of the "Ethiopian" famine but received little aid because the international community regards it as part of Ethiopia. Since 1984-85 Eritreans have faced constant years of drought—including an almost total failure of the rains in 1990, insect infestation which have destroyed meager crops, plus the constant harassment of Ethiopian Mig-23's with their deadly cargoes of cluster bombs and napalm. Yet, the Eritrean Relief Association (ERA), which is wholly Eritrean managed and administered and largely financed by contributions from Eritrean refugees, has grown into the largest indigenous relief operation in Africa simply because non-governmental organizations (NGOs) like Oxfam and BandAid know they can trust their contributions to be used efficiently.

To anyone who visits Eritrea—and many journalists have made the journey—what impresses most is not the military victories or even the survival in the face of indescribable hardship, rather it is the self-reliant, self-financed social revolution which is taking place in one of the poorest, most negatively conservative and backward parts of Africa. The problems are enormous: half of the children die before they are a year old; a quarter of the women die as result of childbirth; simply preventable infectious diseases are common; women, especially in lowland nomadic societies, are less valued than domestic animals; polygamy, infibulation and clitorectomy are widespread; the population is largely illiterate and accepting of traditions which kept land in the hands of a few, impoverished the many and admitted little improvement. Perhaps most destructive was a traditional fatalism which precluded the belief that they could be responsible for their own lives or contribute to the creation of a better society. Military victories against Ethiopia are imperative for survival: victories in the mind will determine the quality of independence.

This book is the Eritreans' story, told where ever possible in their own words, of their remarkable survival as a people and their creation of a new society in the midst of poverty, war and famine. Paradoxically, it is a story of hope rather than despair on a continent where even the most optimistic find hope an elusive emotion.

HISTORICAL BACKGROUND

The Horn of Africa

The Horn of Africa, especially those areas bordering the Red Sea, has attracted traders for more than 5,000 years. Their *dhows* and *feluccas* made their way along the Red Sea coast as far south as Somalia and the Swahili city states of Lamu, Pate and perhaps Zanzibar. They came from Pharonic Egypt, Classical Greece, Persia, the Arabian peninsula and Ottoman Turkey. The ancient port of Adulis (near present day Massawa) was an important trading center for the Empire of Tigre in the Ethiopian highlands in Roman times. For three centuries before they were expelled by the Egyptians in 1875 the Ottoman Turks controlled trade along the Red Sea from their base at Suakin near modern Port Sudan. Until the middle nineteenth century foreign contacts were essentially trade relations which did little to encourage the nine nationalities which make up Eritrea to think of themselves as a national political unit.

In contrast to external contacts, internal historical developments within the Horn of Africa, particularly in Ethiopia and the Sudan served to set Eritrea apart from other regions in the area. The most important of these developments were the rise of the empire of Axum, the importance of the Beja nomads in the Sudan, the rapid spread of Islam and most significantly, the imperial expansion of the Amhara state of Showa in the nineteenth century into the Abyssinian-Ethiopian Empire.

Axum in Ethiopia's Tigre province looks much like any number of provincial towns in Ethiopia. The bullet-pocked King Ezania Hotel testifies to the continuing violence which wracks Tigray as the Tigray People's

Although Eritrea has significant agricultural potential, the EPLF base area, Orota, lies in the arid mountains. Camouflaged under thorn trees and dug into bunkers are the offices, schools, workshops and hospitals which sustain the struggle.

Liberation Front gradually takes control of the province. Overlooking the ruins of what was once the greatest empire in the Horn of Africa, the unfinished five-star state-owned hotel, once intended to bring tourists to Axum, is now the burned out former headquarters of the Ethiopian military command which fled in 1988.

Converted to Christianity in the fourth century by Syrian missionaries, the rulers of Axum created a tributary empire which included Tigray and extended as far as Nubia in the Sudan. Its trading depot, the port of Adulis on the Red Sea, exported the products of the interior and imported the manufactures of the Roman classical world. Until its decline and ultimate disintegration at the end of the ninth century the Axumite empire included most of the Eritrean highlands. Through Axum, Christianity and the ancient *Geez* alphabet spread throughout the highlands of Eritrea. If Christianity gave people a common cultural element, it had little effect on the fierce autonomy of the nationalities.

In 640 A.D. Muslims from the Arabian peninsula crossed the Red Sea to conquer North Africa, Spain, and the Middle East up to the borders of China and India. Arabian traders soon dominated coastal trade, economically strangling the Axumite Empire. Arabs introduced Islam into the Eritrean lowlands where it remains dominant. By the end of the seventh century Eritrea was occupied by the nine different nationalities—Tigre, Tigrinya, Bilen, Afar, Beja, Saho, Baria, Baza and Rashaida—which make up modern Eritrea. Together with "traditional" religions, Coptic Christianity was predominant among highland farmers and Islam among nomadic and semi-nomadic lowlanders. Although Christianity and Islam contributed unifying elements to Eritrea, a significant Eritrean identity was yet to be forged.

The Horn of Africa has today the greatest concentration of nomads anywhere in the world. To see these impoverished desert dwellers today it is easy to forget that they were once among the great powers of the Horn before colonialism, modern economies and new concepts of political power relegated them to the periphery of modern society.

Ethiopia and Eritrea

In recent years the Horn of Africa, especially Ethiopia, has become a symbol of poverty, famine and development aid gone wrong. But in the past Ethiopia meant something quite different to Westerners: a seemingly timeless mountain Christian empire in "pagan" Africa, unconquered, uncolonized, with a rich literary and artistic tradition, isolated, and in Gibbons' famous phrase, "forgetful of the world by whom she was forgotten." Westerners formed their views about Ethiopia based on a general ignorance of Africa and a misunderstanding of Ethiopian history which was fanciful at best and, at worst, outright Ethiopian propaganda designed to promote Emperor Haile Selassie's imperial ambitions in what is still the poorest country on the continent.

Historical Myths

The most fraudulent myth—one which still finds wide acceptance and is at the heart of a continuing internal political crisis—is the claim of the Amhara-speaking ruling class that modern Ethiopia is the direct successor to earlier kingdoms and therefore its modern boundaries reach back to Biblical times, rather than being the creation of the 1890s. To outsiders Ethiopia *seems* ancient but as even elementary historical textbooks show, modern Ethiopia was created by the Amhara-speaking King of Shoa, Menelik II, who was crowned in 1888. Under Menelik, the Amhara, supported by the Coptic Christian Church, became a feudal aristocracy in an imperial Abyssinia (later called Ethiopia) which conquered and colonized surrounding peoples. Amhara history appropriated the achievements of others and became Ethiopian history. The vast majority of the population were referred to as the "minorities" who bitterly resented the expropriation of their land by the Emperor and their forced transformation from free farmers to the tenants of Amhara absentee landlords who exploited them mercilessly and allowed them to starve to death by the millions during times of famine. Perhaps most profoundly, they hated the cultural arrogance of the Amhara who replaced local languages and culture with Amharic and who regarded non-Amharas as beneath respect.

The world is not used to thinking of an African country as an imperialist power: this was a role appropriated by Great Britain, Portugal, France, Germany and Italy. In the 1880s, during the Scramble for Africa, when the continent was divided into colonies, Ethiopia more than doubled in size, defeating Italy in the competition to colonize new lands. In Eritrea Ethiopian imperialism came late—in the 1950s—and while Eritrea's demands for independence have received the widest publicity, in other conquered regions of Ethiopia—in Tigray and in Oromo and parts of Somalia and elsewhere—there are liberation movements also seeking various forms of regional autonomy. In the last three years Ethiopian rule has effectively been overthrown in the province of Tigray, once the site of the ancient

Kingdom of Axum. Oromo fighters have attacked the outskirts of Addis Ababa, a city built on conquered Oromo land. The Ethiopian tragedy is that under its emperors and since 1974, under a leftist dictatorship, it has never been able to make the transition from empire to state.

The Tragedy of Ethiopia

Ethiopia is disintegrating. Its government, whether feudal under Haile Selassie or leftist under Mengistu Haile Mariam, remains dominated by an Amhara elite which refuses to share political power. Ironically independence for Eritrea would only mean a smaller Ethiopia, something to which Addis Ababa could readjust and which would not dramatically alter the structure of political power in Ethiopia. The demands of the Tigrayans, Oromos and others for a federal political system with significant regional autonomy (rather than independence) is much more dangerous to the Amhara because it would mean the end of their political, economic and social domination built up over the past 150 years.

It was the Italian intervention in Africa which set the stage for the current Eritrean tragedy and Eritreans have been deeply disappointed that Italy, for economic reasons, has courted Ethiopia and not taken a leading international role in settling the Eritrean question. Italy was one of the last European states to enter the colonial Scramble for Africa. Between 1882 and 1885 it occupied the ports of Assab and Massawa and by 1890 had created the colony they called Eritrea. Italy intended to use Eritrea as a springboard for expansion into Abyssinia, as Ethiopia was then known. Italian expeditions which pressed into the hinterland struggled against fierce resistance. In 1896 they suffered a crushing defeat on the plains of Adua in Tigray which prevented further incursions into Abyssinia until the rise of fascism. In 1935 Mussolini's Italy sought to avenge the humiliation of Adua and by May of 1936 had conquered Abyssinia. With Italy's defeat in 1941 Haile Selassie returned to Ethiopia and the British, who had major colonial interests in the area, temporarily took over the administration of Eritrea.

The Cold War

As the Cold War intensified and the West became increasingly dependent on Middle Eastern oil flowing through the Suez Canal, the Horn of Africa took on a greater significance to Western policy makers. Exhausted by the war and facing increasing pressure for decolonization in its empire, Britain ended its administration of Eritrea in 1952 at a time United Nations opinion was divided between independence and some form of association with Ethiopia. The Eritrean nationalist movement, which had become a potent force during the Italian period, was demanding independence but the United States Secretary of State, John Foster Dulles, told the United Nations General Assembly in 1952,

"From the point of view of justice, the opinions of the Eritrean people must receive consideration. Nevertheless, the strategic interests of the United States in the Red Sea basin and considerations of security and world peace make it necessary that the country has to be linked to our ally, Ethiopia."

In 1952 the UN General Assembly accepted the federation of Eritrea with Ethiopia. Eritrean fears of unjust Ethiopian administration soon became a reality. By 1959 the American consul in Asmara reported:

"Eritrea is run as a police state in so far as political opposition is concerned .... Devoid of any free or opposition press, and with a populace denied the political and other rights guaranteed to them by their constitution, Eritrea is today anything but the autonomous and democratic 'unit' envisioned by the framers of the United Nations Resolution."

In return for communications and military bases near the Eritrean capital Asmara and along the Red Sea, Ethiopia received substantial American military and development aid as well as political support for its expansionist policies. In 1962 Ethiopia engineered a vote in the Eritrean Assembly which, in violation of UN Resolution 390A (v) ended federation (which only the General Assembly had the right to do) and annexed Eritrea into Ethiopia. The United Nations did nothing. After annexation Ethiopia began a systematic Ethiopianization of Eritrea, whose languages were forbidden in favor of Amharic. Eritreans became yet another "minority" in Haile Selassie's feudal Ethiopia.

Eritrean Nationalism

Haile Selassie had shrewdly used American Cold War fears to continue a longstanding policy of Amhara expansion which had begun in the nineteenth century by his grandfather Menelik. What he did not realize was the

"I hid my two children deep among the corpses, underneath blood soaked sheets...." Amna is one of a few survivors of the 1988 She'eb massacre where four hundred villagers were crushed and machine gunned to death by Ethiopian tanks.

extent to which the colonial experience had created Eritrean nationalism among the country's nine nationalities and the extent to which this was stimulated by the forced annexation. Restricted from entering the professions, especially in the fields of politics and economics, Eritreans concentrated on technical skills, becoming lower level civil servants, skilled mechanics, carpenters, masons and other types of artisans whose skills would ultimately serve the resistance.

Asmara, the capital, was full of young, talented, frustrated Eritreans able to articulate emerging Eritrean demands for self-reliance and independence but with no legitimate political outlet. They saw themselves being colonized at a time when decolonization was taking place everywhere in the third world, especially Africa. Among the most forceful of the new nationalists was Wolde Ab Wolde Miriam who became the spokesman of Eritrean national aspirations, first in Eritrea itself and later in exile in Cairo where he made regular radio broadcasts. The ideas of Wolde Ab fell as rain onto a sponge. Everywhere, especially in the urban areas, his newspaper articles and broadcasts were read, listened to, argued about and used to stimulate further political debate.

Ethiopian annexation drove Eritrean nationalists underground. The failure of the United Nations to enforce its own resolution by refusing to confront Ethiopia over the annexation would lead ultimately to armed resistance and the longest war in contemporary Africa.

Eritreans, then as now, had hopes for a diplomatic resolution. But when the Organization of African Unity (OAU) was created in 1964, two years after the annexation of Eritrea, its first meeting was held in Addis Ababa under the chairmanship of Africa's elder statesman, Emperor Haile Selassie. One of the OAU's first orders of business was to declare the present boundaries of African states as inviolate. Haile Selassie was successful in portraying the Eritreans as "secessionists" dangerous to the "ancient" unity of Ethiopia, while the Eritreans, without representation at the OAU, were unable to bring Eritrea forward as a colonial question. Governments worldwide accepted the OAU's border policy and Eritrea ceased to exist, sacrificed to the geopolitical imperatives of the Cold War.

The Armed Struggle

Within Eritrea the armed struggle began in 1962 shortly after annexation when a few desperate nationalists turned revolutionaries managed to steal two pistols and attacked a police station. Initially organized as the Eritrean Liberation Front (ELF) the resistance movement grew quickly but fractionalized into a number of groups, principally the Eritrean Liberation Front (ELF) and the Eritrean

People's Liberation Front (EPLF). The two groups fought a bloody civil war in the 1970s. The ELF is no longer a fighting force in Eritrea, and many of its members are now members of the EPLF. Between 1962 and 1977 the EPLF and ELF took control of 90 percent of Eritrea making a mockery of Ethiopia's claim to effectively govern the "province."

Within Ethiopia enormous changes were also taking place: Emperor Haile Selassie, whose government had viewed the tragic famine of 1972-73 as the inevitable, periodic fate of the peasantry and which had done too little too late to relieve the suffering, was overthrown and replaced by the Marxist government of Mengistu Haile Mariam. Ironically, the Dergue, as the government became known, promised that no such tragedy would ever be allowed to take place again. The United States was forced out and its influence replaced by the Soviet Union which, aided by Cuba, expanded and trained the Ethiopian army to crush the Eritrean revolution. Massive inputs of Soviet military equipment flowed into Ethiopia, most importantly Mig-23 fighter-bombers equipped with cluster bombs and napalm. Superpower support for

A soldier waits in the trenches which separated Ethiopian and Eritrean troops for a decade: his water container is an unexploded bomb shell once intended to kill him.

the Dergue temporarily tilted the balance of military power. After the once prosperous agricultural town of Nacfa was destroyed by Ethiopian airpower, the Eritreans, lacking air defenses, abandoned the towns and parts of the countryside in what they call the Strategic Withdrawal, and built an impregnable base area where they fought a classic guerrilla war. Since 1978 Ethiopia has launched annual Soviet planned offensives. In 1982 Ethiopia committed all its military resources—troops, airpower, navy—to the massive Red Star offensive, to "crush the bandits" (as they call the Eritreans) only to be routed. In 1984-85 offensives continued against a desperate, starving population. International food aid for Eritrea, which was at the epicenter of the famine, was given, for political reasons, to Ethiopia. Famine and food became instruments of war; food intended by the international community for Eritrea, 90% of which was in the hands of the EPLF, was sold by the Ethiopian military to traders who transported it to Sudan or withheld it from suspected EPLF supporters.

Ethiopian offensives have been systematically defeated by EPLF fighters. For the past decade 250 miles of trenches, similar to WWI, have separated the EPLF and Ethiopian armies. Since 1984, the EPLF has captured enough Soviet supplied tanks to defeat the Ethiopians in classic tank battles. In 1988 the EPLF broke through the trenches and destroyed the Ethiopian garrison at the town of Afabet capturing large numbers of new Russian T-55 main battle tanks, 130mm howitzers, and mountains of ammunition. In February 1990 they captured the port of Massawa and encircled the capital, Asmara. The huge Ethiopian Second Revolutionary Army is facing total defeat. Ethiopian prisoners of war now number nearly 50,000.

Because of its political isolation the EPLF been forced to rely almost entirely on its own resources not only to survive the war but also to implement their concept of self-reliant development. It has created a remarkable selflessness amongst traditionally fiercely individualistic people, who now see tangible, practical improvements in their lives though education, medicine as well as the possibility for a better future. They borrow no money and have no debts—the EPLF is financed by regular contributions from Eritrean refugees who believe in the EPLF's military, social and economic goals. No salaries are paid—to anyone—from the Secretary General to the soldier in field. The buildup of infrastructure in EPLF-controlled areas—again estimated at between 80-90 percent of Eritrea—is planned and carried out by Eritreans rather than imported experts. Relief efforts during the famine and longer term humanitarian development aid are the responsibility of the Eritrean Relief Association (ERA).

Self reliance has been forced upon Eritrea and they have made it a virtue. They have survived against incalculable odds—through a generation of war, years of drought and the horrors of famine. Not only are they surviving but they have created the seeds of a new state and a new society which will be of interest to anyone concerned with development problems of the Third World. The story of Eritrea raises all of the fundamental questions of development—the role of the state and individual; the appropriate structure of the economy of a developing country; appropriate ways of creating public health care, education, infrastructure planning, the struggle to reconcile the positive elements of tradition with a modern state, relations with the power blocks of the international community. Perhaps what has impressed visitors to Eritrea most is the sheer indomitable will of the Eritrean people unwilling to give up their belief that by relying upon themselves they can survive to create a better society.

Ahmed and his family live a semi-nomadic life in the EPLF base area at Orota.

TRADITIONS

"We are oppressed by the Ethiopians, but we are also oppressed by our own traditions."

Nomads and Farmers

Ahmed and his family live in the nomadic tradition in the center of the EPLF's Orota base area. His pair of plastic EPLF fighters' sandals are his only concession to modern dress. As we climb to the top of a nearby hill, Ahmed laughs easily as he explains that his family has always lived in this area. He knows the name of every mountain, canyon and gully: every significant feature of the landscape. He points out places which, to an untrained eye seem identical to the surrounding arid, rocky mountains, where goats can be grazed for a day or two, especially if there has been sufficient air moisture in the evenings to stimulate the growth of grass and shrubs. With such knowledge Ahmed is able to maintain his goats throughout the year. Like all nomadic communities Ahmed's survival is extremely vulnerable to drought. "If drought comes," he explains, "it is God's will. If we die that is also God's will."

My guide, Yosief, shakes his head slowly and glances at me as if to say: "These are the traditional attitudes we want to change; to take away the fatalism and make people believe they can take control of their lives." When asked how traditionalism and revolution combine, Yosief, explains:

"We have nine nationalities in Eritrea—roughly divided between lowland nomads and highland farmers. In each nationality there are changes we would like to make—land reform, improve the position of women, better hygiene, agricultural techniques; I could give you a very long list. We can only teach by example not by coercion; we try to show nomadic families the benefits of a more settled life but they are free to choose how they live. They are individualists; you cannot coerce them to change. They will just walk away."

Ahmed's family is encamped nearby; their tent a patchwork of bits of cloth and old food aid bags, a

Left: Male nomad children tend the goat herds at an early age. Ahmed's family is attempting to rebuild their herd after a series of disastrous droughts and famines. Above: Traditionally women live in subservience to men, their social contacts limited to their immediate family.

testimony to their impoverishment, the result of the recent famine and the continuing drought. Whatever wealth Ahmed had has long been sold to survive the famine. Having lost most of his animals in the famine of 1984-85 he has begun to rebuild the herd but the total failure of the rains in 1990 will impoverish him again. He has the good fortune to live with the EPLF which means he can draw water from the EPLF-supplied holding tanks which are filled each night by self built tanker trucks and he can be reached by emergency food distributions. Most nomadic families are too scattered and too remote to benefit from such help and they bear the brunt of famine.

Ahmed's son Ali herds the goats during the day. He is curious about the cameras and follows me around remaining at a distance and saying nothing. At ten years old he already has the stoicism of his tradition; when he steps onto a two inch long acacia thorn, he makes no sound, hobbles to his uncle's tent, has it extracted and then scampers away. Although primary education is available in this area through the EPLF Ahmed sees no purpose in sending Ali to school: he is needed at home.

*Top, Opposite: Considered unworthy of education, women were expected to spend their lives secluded in their tents content with domestic routines. "Just as there is no donkey with horns, so there is no woman with brains," runs one Eritrean proverb. **Above:** Eager for modern medical treatment offered by the EPLF, this nomad woman assumes her traditional social role which does not permit a woman to look directly at a man.*

Miriam, Ahmed's wife, offers to prepare us coffee (to be served by her husband). Aside from brief periods of travel where she will be carried secluded on the camel, Miriam will spend virtually all of her life in the tent. She personifies the nomad axiom that "A woman enters her tent on the day she is married and leaves it the day she dies." She is intensely shy, especially around men, but her contacts with the fighters and examples of liberated women around her has reduced her isolation. She was betrothed as a child and married at puberty. She lives in a society which practices polygamy, female circumcision and infibulation. She is illiterate and totally economically dependent on her husband. But she is well treated according to her tradition and it would wrong to assume she is unhappy. Ahmed is a generous man and they live in an area where their physical survival is assured and where they have access to EPLF health services which many women value, especially nomadic women where one in four die as a result of childbirth using traditional medicine. They already see

some of the benefits of a more sedentary life. Although it is difficult to imagine Ahmed ever giving up nomadism, clearly he and his family are already beginning to adjust their lives to the new possibilities the EPLF offers.

Although nomadism is regarded by most national governments as anachronistic and nomadic communities have found it most difficult to adjust and participate in the new states of the Horn, there are vast desert areas, including parts of Eritrea, which are only suitable to nomadic or semi-nomadic economies.

Among the largely Muslim nomadic or semi-nomadic pastoralists of the lowlands a different type of society developed from that in the settled, agriculturalist highlands. The nomads practice a form of Islam which on the one hand can appear naive because of its simplicity and lack of concern with the ideological-theological factionalism which has divided Muslims into Sunnis, Shias and others, but on the other it remains deeply true to Islam's essential teachings.

Men's work—ploughing and herding—was seen as central to both the agricultural and nomadic economies but women's work was trivialized.

Sadly for women, pre-Islamic practices of circumcision and infibulation are widely believed to be required by devout Muslims. Although there are exceptions among Eritrea's nine nationalities, women's lives in both Islamic and Christian societies were particularly circumscribed by domestic routines, exclusion from civic affairs and the trading economy and by their limited social and legal status. Generally women were not allowed to own land, engage in trade, work at skilled crafts like weaving or sewing; socially they spoke only when spoken to and dared never contradict a man or look directly into his face.

Socially nomadic societies were even more stratified than the agriculturalists. A small elite often dominated a large majority of subordinates and slaves (formally abolished in the 1940s) who had no say in the civil affairs of the community but who had substantial financial, labor and social obligations which bound them to a particular master or family. The position of women tended to be even more restrictive: women were essentially the property

of men who joke: "We love our animals more than our women." In any case women are easier to replace than livestock—and often cheaper.

Political power rested in a few hands or in a chief who decided on behalf of the group. Given its assumptions this ancient system effectively governed nomadic societies but attempts to alter it were repressed with violence or exile. The authoritarian political tradition of nomadic Eritrea would haunt the early attempts of Eritrean nationalists to organize against Ethiopian colonization and would play a major role in the EPLF splitting from the largely traditionalist Muslim ELF and the subsequent brief, bitter, civil war of the early 1970s.

In the highlands, settled agriculturalist village communities developed and were overwhelmingly Coptic Christian. They were essentially patriarchies controlled by men; women were not permitted to participate in civil affairs and were not entitled to own land or to engage in trade or other economic activities.

At the Janni market, women bargain for the silver jewelry necessary for marriage.

In the morning mist a farmer ploughs his stony field; his first crop failed, this one will also fail. Impoverishment, decades of drought and land degradation have left formerly self sufficient farmers chronically hungary and facing regular famine.

Above: In the past decade, farmers in the highlands have rarely had normal rainfall. *Next page:* This young shepherd ignores the pain of removing a 2-inch-long acacia thorn from his foot.

The Eritrean highlands are comparatively densely populated and the fertility of the land varies significantly. During the Italian colonial period large numbers of impoverished farmers abandoned their marginal plots to work on the new Italian commercial farms and in the new industrial-urban areas of Eritrea, thereby further weakening production of the peasant agricultural sector.

Traditional Eritrean societies were almost entirely rural, dependent on their religious traditions for the little education which existed in the form of Koranic schools or Coptic monastery schools. The weight of continuity made change exceptionally difficult even though the vast majority of people experienced extreme poverty and vulnerability to drought and famine. A religiously inspired fatalism combined with a limited medical knowledge offered Eritreans a life expectancy of 38 years and a 50 percent infant mortality rate. The overwhelming majority were illiterate and among women illiteracy was 90-95 percent.

In seeking to make fundamental social changes in Eritrea the EPLF faces, as do all Third World governments, a deeply conservative traditionalism. The EPLF is committed to modernizing Eritrean society without ignoring its traditions and destroying it essential character. During the Italian colonial period Eritrean traditions were wholly ignored and assumed to have no relevance. Basic education for Eritreans was described in 1932 by the Director of Education as:

"By the end of the fourth year, the Eritrean student should be able to speak our language moderately well, he should know the four arithmetical operations . . . he should be a convinced propagandist of the principles of hygiene, and of history, he should know only the names of those who have made Italy great."

But even this limited and biased education together with the experience of colonial subjugation created a group of Eritreans who could visualize the potential of their society. Eritrean nationalism was born. It sought, then as now, the political freedom to apply a new vision of society to the whole of Eritrea. The nationalists accepted a tremendous responsibility; to develop the improvements a modern society can offer and to make the personal commitment to start the process of transforming traditional societies. There is no simple model for doing this; Eritrean nationalists have sought examples in each of the political-economic systems of our time—capitalist democracies, socialist democracies, single party socialist states—anywhere there seemed to be help in forging the tools for modernizing society. As one fighter told me:

"How naive we were twenty years ago when we thought we could change Eritrea quickly just by telling or showing people a better way. Obviously this did not work and now we understand that transforming Eritrea's traditions will take generations. We have learned from our failures and we have learned from the failures of others."

A highland family struggles to bring their sick child to an EPLF clinic. Half of Eritrea's population of 3.5 million are children under 18: 40-70 percent are malnourished; nearly half die before age five.

Each blade of grass selected and picked by hand. Without supplementary food aid delivered by the Eritrean Relief Association (ERA), highland farmers would be forced to abandon their land and become refugees or urban squatters in nearby Sudan.

CHALLENGE

*"There are two challenges:
the challenge to survive
and the challenge to create
a new society."*

His spelling is imperfect—but this fighter spends a part of each day improving his English, part of the basic education given to all fighters, even those in the frontlines.

POLITICS
OF
INDEPENDENCE

*"Eritrea is not a
secessionist problem.
It is an unresolved
colonial question."*

WE SHALL BEAT OUR SWORDS INTO PLOWS

Professor of International Law and former attorney general of Ethiopia, Bereket Habte Selassie, now EPLF representative in the United States, is attempting to bring the Eritrean question before a reluctant United Nations.

Professorial, greying, 50ish, distinguished, Bereket Habte Selassie has spent his professional career seeking justice for his homeland. He divides his time between Washington, D.C., where he is professor of International Politics and Law at Howard and Georgetown Universities, and New York City, where he represents the EPLF at the United Nations.

As he lights his pipe he explains, "I was educated in England. I took law degrees at the Universities of London and Hull and I earned a Ph.D. in African Constitutional Law at the University of London. I worked in various capacities as a lawyer in Ethiopia between 1956 and 1964, after Eritrea became federated to Ethiopia. At that time all Eritreans became Ethiopian nationals so therefore there was an interesting situation in which Eritreans were obliged to work in the government. I started as a legal counsel in the government, eventually becoming the Attorney General of Ethiopia in

1961. I resigned in 1964 mainly in protest over the Eritrean question.

"My position is anomalous; at the United Nations you are either the head of a mission representing a government or you are an observer. Organizations like the African National Congress have observer status in the United Nations; we don't even have *that* status even though we are historically and legally the responsibility of the United Nations. This is an argument supported by the historical and legal facts. This is not propaganda: the information is available to anyone who cares to read the United Nations resolutions.

"The United Nations is directly responsible for the current situation in Eritrea. It created the federation with Ethiopia under which we were supposed to have local autonomy and it took no action when we were

In 1987, after a decade of dissension and a period of near civil war, the EPLF and the ELF joined forces during a unity congress in the Orota base area attended by representatives of European, Middle Eastern and African governments and political parties. Hundreds of delegates assembled to elect new leadership and set the EPLF agenda for the next five years.

unilaterally and illegally annexed by Emperor Haile Selassie in 1962. Let me read you a part of a secret report to the State Department by Richard Johnson, the American consul in Eritrea, which we have obtained under the Freedom of Information Act.

"The 'unification' [of Eritrea with Ethiopia] was prepared and perpetrated from above in maximum secrecy without the slightest public debate of discussion. The 'vote of acclamation' [in the Eritrean Parliament] was a shoddy comedy . . . .

"We feel we are entitled—legally, morally and historically—to be represented at the United Nations."

"Look at you! You've gotten old while we have remained to fight and stayed young!" chides old friend, Tamu, who has lost three sons in the war. Wolde Ab Wolde Mariam, the "Father of Eritrean Nationalism," returned to EPLF-controlled Eritrea in 1987 to be greeted as a hero. More than anyone else Wolde Ab symbolizes Eritrea's long struggle for independence. Left: Everywhere he appeared in Eritrea, fighters came to hear him.

"Eritrea Is an Unresolved Colonial Question: We Are Not a Secessionist Movement"

"Eritrea is a colonial question which has been forgotten: it is not a secessionist question. We do not want to see the disintegration of Ethiopia. Over the last few years, as the Eritrean story has become better known through the drought, famine and war and as we have also redoubled our efforts to inform the international community, you would be surprised to know how many people, including ambassadors, have admitted that they were unaware that Eritrea was formerly an Italian colony. Many policy makers mistakenly regard Eritrea as a historical part of

In order to foster unity among Eritrea's nine nationalities and demonstrate the gains made in gender relationships, women dancers, who formerly would never have performed in public, entertain the Congress. **Right:** *As Jean Victor Nkolo of the BBC French Service interviews Congress guests from Europe, Ethiopian Antonov bombers flying photographic missions come under EPLF anti-aircraft fire.*

Ethiopia when even a rudimentary knowledge of the area demonstrates this is simply untrue.

"We are hopeful African countries and others will eventually say, 'This is not a secession; this is a legitimate question of a nation which has been denied its independence, let us debate it in the U.N.' Unfortunately the official position of the Organization of African Unity, which other countries look to for guidance in their relations with Africa, accepts the principle that we are a secessionist movement. They put it this way: 'Eritrea is an integral part of Ethiopia and my government is not at liberty, under any circumstances, to intervene in the domestic affairs of a member country whether it is an OAU member or a UN member.'

Above: During the Unity Congress, women from the Solomuna refugee camp play traditional and modern music on self made and donated instruments.

"Legally and historically, right and justice are on our side. But how do you convince others who might not have the interest or the time, or for political reasons choose to ignore justice, to put this on their agenda? This has been our problem. Look at the Americans for instance: they accuse us of not only being secessionists but also Marxists. When the Americans denied our right to self-determination in the 1950s there was nothing to secede from; we had been an Italian colony liberated by Italy's defeat in World War II. And as for Marxism, I don't think the word 'Marxism' had ever been heard in Eritrea. So it wasn't clearly ideology—Marxism or whatever—that caused them to deny us independence. Strategic interests prompted US policy makers to deny us a hearing. Even now many American policy makers are naively hopeful that after the excesses of the Mengistu government in the name of socialism, Ethiopia, including Eritrea, will return to the Western camp."

A sceptical John Kifner, New York Times *Middle Eastern Bureau Chief, interviews EPLF Secretary General Isaias Afwerki.*

At the Nacfa Front EPLF fighters rush to their firing positions along the 250 miles of trenches which divided the Eritrean and Ethiopian armies for a decade.

THE WAR
FOR
INDEPENDENCE

*"The scar starts just
above the eye,
tearing its way the length
of the face to the
point of the chin."*

Captured at Afabet in 1988, a 130mm howitzer hurls its deadly missile nine miles onto the Ethiopian garrison defending Keren, one of only two towns left in Ethiopian hands. After thirty years, Africa's oldest war continues.

In the 113-degree heat of Khartoum, Sudan, surrounded by the fragrance of sweet tea and an incongruous Alpine mural painted on the tea-room wall, Semere shrugs off my question about the scar and begins to brief me about the war in Eritrea.

"It started so long ago; I was just a child. Who could believe it would last so long? We are weary of war but if we have to fight for another generation we will do it—*never* misunderstand that.

"As you already know, the Ethiopians call us 'bandits' as if we had no political goals; even the BBC calls us 'rebels' when they know that we were illegally annexed and are fighting for our independence. It has been difficult for us to reach the outside world in a way which allows them to understand the true situation in Eritrea.

"We face the third largest army in Africa, which is supported by a superpower, the Soviet Union, and its allies. The Soviets and the East Germans provided the Ethiopians with huge amounts of military aid. But the

Once a small guerrilla force, the EPLF has developed into what has been called "the most effective guerrilla army in the world."

Ethiopian army is made up mostly of conscripted peasants who are filled with lies about Eritreans—told we are Muslim bandits trying to steal their country, take their women and destroy their traditions. They are uneducated and they believe these things. The Soviets equip them well but they are badly trained and badly officered and they have little morale. Our fighters are highly motivated and extremely well trained—at least 20 percent are women—even in the front lines. All are volunteers, none are paid—from our commanders on down. Their stamina and commitment are remarkable; many have been in the front lines for five years and more. They know that if wounded everything will be done to save them. If they are killed they will be properly buried, not left on the field of battle like their Ethiopian counterparts.

"We have defeated the Ethiopians, despite their Soviet weapons and advisors, time after time. In 1982 they attempted to crush us in their now infamous Red Star Campaign where they used 100,000 troops—15 divisions—supported by Migs and helicopter gunships. Not only did we hold, we also killed or wounded a third of their troops and captured large amounts of materiel. This is the way we supply our own forces—with captured weapons—they are our only source of supply. We are able to rebuild and recondition all of the equipment we capture, from Kalashnikov (AK-47) rifles to main battle tanks: when necessary we translate captured repair manuals from Russian into Tigrinya. We recycle everything we capture: the Soviet-supplied boots are a pre-

cious source of leather and are cut up and made into cartridge cases, belts, etc., ammunition boxes become school furniture and building materials. You will see how we use the big Zil 6-wheel-drive trucks to help pull food convoys across the rivers.

"After another decade of fighting we again control about 90 percent of Eritrea. We have captured many prisoners of war [1990 estimates run to 50,000] including Soviet advisors. At times we have had to release prisoners because we did not have the resources to look after them properly. This was especially true during the famine when we released more than 5,000 prisoners. Until recently we received no aid from the Red Cross because the war didn't 'exist' for the international community because the Ethiopia government refused to acknowledge that a full-scale war is taking place in Eritrea. Released prisoners were given the choice of returning to Ethiopia (where they would probably be conscripted again or arrested as deserters), going to a third country—usually Sudan, or remaining in Eritrea: they have chosen all of these options. We treat prisoners of war humanely: they receive basically the same rations as our fighters and they are also given elementary education. The Ethiopian peasant soldiers we capture are not our enemy; they are the victims of a dictatorial state. How can we treat them badly?

"In contrast, in Ethiopia, Eritrean prisoners are routinely murdered and most fighters prefer to take their own lives rather than fall into the hands of the Ethiopi-

ans. Perhaps you have seen some of the photographs we have found on captured Ethiopians, showing Eritreans being tortured or murdered or severed heads spiked onto the bumpers of trucks.

"We had basically defeated the Ethiopians before the Soviets intervened in 1978—we controlled 90 percent of the country and were preparing the necessary administrative structures to govern Eritrea. Soviet support of Ethiopia, especially the Mig aircraft, but also the massive buildup of the Ethiopian army meant we had to give up territory in what we call the Strategic Withdrawal. We could not defend the towns against air attack.

"Our basic support comes from the Eritrean population—inside and outside of Eritrea—and we make every effort to protect them from risk—we could not have survived for a generation without this support. The EPLF civilian departments provide basic services to the rural population; we in the EPLA (Eritrean People's Liberation Army) attempt to protect them from Ethiopian reprisals and minimize their exposure to risks. The military situation is changing all of the time, especially now as we are on the offensive after a decade of holding

In spite of the fact that the Ethiopian army is at least ten times larger than the EPLF and has enjoyed a decade of massive military support from the Soviet Union, EPLF fighters are in control of 90 percent of Eritrea. Many frontline troops are women.

largely defensive positions. But what I have told you should give some idea of the war and why we will ultimately win."

Soviet Intervention

"We would have won our independence in 1978," Bereket explains, "had the Soviet Union not intervened and given the Ethiopian government more than a billion dollars in military aide and advice. We had captured virtually all of the towns and the countryside was entirely in our hands. Now the Soviet Union understands, after a decade of unsuccessful offensives against us, that it is impossible for the Ethiopians to defeat the EPLF and they are trying to persuade Mengistu to deal politically. If that happens then we will be one step closer to recognition of our case."

With John Kifner, Middle Eastern Bureau chief of the *New York Times*, we wait to interview Isaias Afwerki, Secretary General of the EPLF at the EPLF headquarters deep in one of the rugged, dry mountain valleys of northern Eritrea. Afwerki arrives alone on foot and apologizes for making us wait explaining that we have come on a very busy day when he is in important meetings. Months later I would discover that the EPLF military offensives which would play a major role in forcing Ethiopia to negotiations were being planned that day. In his early forties, Isaias, as he is called following the Eritrean custom of using only the first name, is wearing a sport shirt, plastic sandals and worn trousers. Soft spoken to the point of shyness, he speaks thoughtfully and candidly.

Origins of Eritrean Nationalism

"In a small area as diverse as this with nine languages, two major religions, Eritrean nationalism developed largely as a result of foreign intervention. Not all Eritreans share my views but I am convinced that nationalism becomes stronger when there is an external element. The social, cultural, traditional formation of Eritrean society is no different from other societies in Africa, or other underdeveloped countries. People come to a cohesive relationship when there is an external dilemma compelling them to have common feelings, common attitudes: this was basically cultivated by the Italians. Maybe the history up to the coming of Europeans colonialism has its impact in a way but trying to go back thousands of years in search of Eritrean nationalism is not viable when one discusses present national feelings. Recent history—since the beginning of this century—has played a vital role in bringing people together and making them feel the same. After the Second World War the fact that Eritrea was officially denied the right to exercise self determination created a political sentiment of trying to assert one's self as a nation—perhaps even more so than

An EPLF unit moves quickly towards the frontlines at Keren. Each soldier carries one hand grenade: to fight with and, if necessary, to take one's own life. **Right:** EPLF fighters know that if captured they will be tortured, raped and murdered.

the repression of Haile Selassie's regime. I think it accumulated out of these external factors. This is controversial, what I am saying. Others have an historical explanation for Eritrean nationalism which extends into the distant past but I don't agree with this analysis. I trace this development to Italian colonialism, the repression of the Haile Selassie years and now to the repression of the present regime which is worse than that of Haile Selassie. The more people feel they are subjugated; the more you try to assert your common humanity.

"The Italians wanted to create an empire in this area. They had ambitions in North Africa, Europe and of course here. During the Italian period there was an attempt to build a solid infrastructure to be used as a springboard for expansion into the Horn of Africa. I think the efforts of the Italians to create this base transformed the social fabric here in Eritrea. People from different corners of Eritrea who previously had very few historical ties or common political or economic interests were brought together. Of course repression was also a part of Italian colonialism and we shared this experience as Eritreans; segregation was there—all sorts of discrimi-

natory colonial regulations; but their main aims were to use this area for expansion into the Horn and secondarily that Eritrea would become a home for Italians. Many peasants from Sicily and southern Italy were encouraged to migrate to Eritrea."

Political Ideology of the EPLF

"In the first place it is nationalistic; the struggle for political independence. The second element of this nationalism is the aspiration to transform this society into an advanced society in every respect; in industry, agriculture, social relations. People aspire to have a better living condition than they have now. This is the core of the ideology of the EPLF. There were other external influences of course; the 1960s had their influence on the Eritrean struggle; the 1970s had their influences as did the 1980s, now we are in the 1990s—over the decades there have been many ideological transformations. It would be fair to say that we have a more mature attitude towards dealing with external influences now than twenty years ago. There has been an elabora-

Fighters carry njera, *a fermented millet bread which is the staple food, to comrades on Den-Den mountain.* **Below:** *The EPLF fights with captured and recycled weapons: a typical equipment belt fabricated from captured Soviet supplied boots.*

tion of our ideology based on our own experiences during the last two decades. We have to be very practical in dealing with ideology. We won't be spoon fed from outside; we have to look critically at the experiences of others. I think it proper to categorize the ideology of the EPLF in this way because there is too much misunderstanding; people describe the EPLF as being a Marxist organization which is not true. People try to fix the EPLF and its ideology into right-wing or leftist categories which we continuously reject. These things are said by people who are ignorant of the EPLF or of how things have been developing here. When the EPLF is described as a Marxist organization this is done to find a pretext for justifying being against the political rights of the Eritrean people for strategic reasons. Until recently some East bloc governments denounced us as right-wingers in order to make the same justifications. Our experience with ideology is more mature than outsiders want to believe."

Bereket adds, "This is like Alice in Wonderland: if I say this glass is red it is going to be red (even though it is not). This is the Alice in Wonderland principle at work in international politics. The United States makes charges that the EPLF is a Marxist organization. At the same time the Soviet Union says the EPLF is right-wing. There is an utter lack of principle behind these policy statements. The EPLF is self-confident and self-reliant:

Wrapped in his homespun cotton shawl, a fighter who has already lost an eye in battle mans his position in the trenches on Den-Den mountain. The Ethiopians are only thirty yards away.

perhaps big nations don't like this kind of self-reliance. They want smaller nations to be more pliant; to belong ideologically, emotionally and otherwise to one or the other of the superpowers. The EPLF is essentially a democratic nationalist organization which seeks independence for its people. What kind of politics or government the Eritreans will have after independence is up to the Eritrean people to determine through their elected parliament. We are not there yet.

"The EPLF is a broad-based democratic movement for independence. Within this broad-based democratic movement we have our share of Marxists; we have social-democrats; we have conservatives; we have Christians and Muslims. It has been very important for us to refine, deepen and expand democratic principles of plurality. For example, we do not practice 'cult of personality' politics; our leaders are elected democratically for fixed periods. We are nationalists because we have to create a nation out of nine different nationalities. Democratic because we have to have democracy if we are going to succeed. And I think we have succeeded so far. We have learned from the mistakes of rigid socialist ex-

The EPLF attempts to provide everyone in Eritrea with basic education. Frontline troops spend part of each day learning to read and write in their own language, English and Arabic. Equally remarkable is their acceptance of a woman teacher.

perimentation in other parts of Africa and elsewhere. Most of us tend to be social-democratic in terms of social-economic goals for our people. We recognize the limitations of state intervention. But we also recognize the hazards of letting unrestricted market capitalism hold sway in our country. So we have to find, when the time comes, the optimal way of creating a socio-economic system which will benefit the people. These arguments of right-wingism or Marxism are red herrings. One can only think in terms of ideals: an independent Eritrea would embrace opportunity for *all* social groups and political tendencies. How that can be achieved is difficult to predict but as an ideal it is a part of our position. We talk about a mixed economy: having a private and public sector. Their relationships—the percentage of the economy of each sector, how the private sector would be regulated; what would be the involvement of external parties; how much would the government manage; how much in the private sector. There are different schools of thought but concrete programs and policies are premature to formulate at this stage. But these are our goals. We are particularly proud that we have been able

Frontline volleyball: a punctured ball and a tattered net. Just over the hill Ethiopian snipers wait.

to survive against all odds. We are increasingly self-reliant but it has been a long process with many mistakes—but we have developed a proficiency to survive."

Transformation of Society

"When one comes to socially transforming the society," Isaias continues, "in the 1960s one was easily convinced that intensive political work—raising the awareness of the population—would transform their attitudes quickly. It was so easy to think in terms of politics and assume that you could bring change within a matter of years. Sometimes we thought we could mobilize the population in a matter of months and transform the social fabric of the society quickly. We have been doing this for quite some time—more than a quarter century—and we have not achieved anything like what we had hoped. This has been a sobering experience and we are constantly seeking ways to improve. This is a very gradual process. You can't just tell a simple farmer or pastoralist to come and look at this house and dream of building a house like this. He *never* has had this idea in his mind. He wants to live in his thatch house; he does not want to change and he dislikes the luxury of life. Why? Nobody can tell that. That is the way he thinks. You can tell him this is better; it is cooler, better ventilated, healthier, but he does not want to live in this kind of house and he does

A cultural troup entertains frontline fighters with skits portraying their victory over the Ethiopians. Such groups not only entertain troops, they also seek to break down prejudices created by isolation and promote unity between Eritrea's nationalities.

War shatters families: Saba's brother is a member of the Dergue, the Ethiopian government she is fighting. A nurse at Orota hospital, she offers the "Father of Eritrea," Wolde Ab Wolde Mariam, the traditional smell of roasting coffee beans.

not have the idea of working hard to build such a house. We have no interest in forcing him to do this. We formulate programs and policies to change the economy, the life style of the population, to make people more productive, to transform pastoralists into agriculturalists. But all this does not happen in a matter of months or years; it takes decades. We have learned this the hard way. But we have gained a lot of experience in the last decades and we have been transforming as individuals; we have not been sticking to old ideals trying to implement them whatever the obstacles; this has not been a tradition of the EPLF.

"When you are in a struggle to survive and you are denied all help you utilize whatever resources you have in order to survive and continue. We are self-reliant. It is the cornerstone of our ideology. We have a considerable number of educated and skilled people in our society—compared with other groups in this region. The existence of skilled people has allowed us to tackle many problems without external help. To buy a truck is expensive but relatively simple, but if you are not able to maintain that truck, in a short time it is ruined and this we cannot afford. When you have skilled people you can get as much out of this truck as possible. We have to solve problems with our skills because we have very little money.

"When it comes to the military aspect of the struggle the EPLF also relies on self reliance. In the early days of the ELF, before the emergence of the EPLF, we started by attacking some police station or going and attacking a depot somewhere in Asmara trying to collect

weapons because there was no alternative; you won't survive if you have to depend on arms from outsiders. We learned this early. From this beginning we have now captured main battle tanks, military vehicles, ammunition, thousands of assault rifles, heavy artillery—all supplied by the Soviets to Ethiopia to crush us as a people. In many ways this question of necessity has made the EPLF successful. Without the element of self-reliance—the desire for people to survive and assert themselves as a nation—it could not have been achieved. Without the support of the people we couldn't survive. We find many societies with a large number of educated and skilled people who have not been able to transform themselves. They rely too heavily on outside help to do things they should do themselves."

Financing the EPLF

Bereket explains, "The EPLF is financed entirely by contributions from its members. Eritreans in the diaspora—not all of them—but a substantial number of them—contribute regularly, monthly to the EPLF. This is the main source of the EPLF's income. They believe in what we do and we are accountable to them. In times of challenge, when there is an offensive or a famine, regular Eritrean evenings or campaigns seek special contributions—what we call the *Kitet* which means 'tightening your belt for the cause.' In the United States such a *Kitet* can raise two million dollars in a few months—we make similar appeals in Europe, the Middle East and Africa. In times of crisis, such as during the famine, or for certain development projects contributions have been made by non-governmental organizations (NGOs) or by friendly governments, in particular in the Gulf, but these are for humanitarian-developmental reasons. The EPLF does not receive financial help from governments; we depend on our own people."

"I am an idealist," says Bereket, "I have a family myself—when I see the living conditions of the pastoralists—well, it is deplorable. Many of them died during the famine because they were so vulnerable. Half of their children die in the first years and many women die in childbirth. We are not against traditional values but we want to offer people the chance to make improvements in their lives. When you come from an urban area, have the advantages of education and a broader perspective; this creates a certain responsibility to others who have not enjoyed these advantages."

A Call for Free Elections

"The EPLF's position has always been clear on the question of a peaceful settlement. Our fathers demanded their right to peaceful self-determination, expecting the international community (particularly the UN) to hear them and give them justice. When that did not happen the creation of the armed struggle was the inevitable result. It should be understood that the Eritrean armed struggle is supported by the entire Eritrean nation.

Forced by Ethiopian airpower—against which they have no effective defense—to live in underground bunkers and to restrict their movements during the day, Eritreans nevertheless manage to enjoy the pleasure of afternoon coffee, often laced with pungent ginger. Next Page: The commitment to educational improvement is remarkable—everywhere people are studying, even in bunkers at the front.

Nevertheless we have always said that we are not out in the field because of any love of carrying arms. We know the cost of that. I don't think anyone can claim to know that better than we do—what this means for our people in terms of suffering, death, destruction of property and dislocation of people. The refugee population of Eritreans inside and outside of Eritrea is now nearing the million mark—almost a third of our population! Nearly 600,000 live in the Sudan, most of them under appalling conditions; some 80,000 are settled in Saudi Arabia and the Gulf with a further 25,000 in Europe and America."

"We are not interested in peace as a matter of tactics; we really want peace. In November of 1980 the EPLF proposed a peaceful solution; a decade later we stand by our proposal. The essence is that an internationally supervised referendum should be organized under which the Eritrean people should be asked to choose between local autonomy within an Ethiopian framework, some kind of federation with Ethiopia or, complete independence. Let the Eritrean people decide. In 1980 this was not favorably received by the Ethiopians and ten years later it is the same. The reasons are quite clear: they know Eritreans would vote for independence, despite official propaganda that the majority of Eritreans wish to remain within Ethiopia. Their response to our proposal was a series of major military

offensives, all of which have failed. Our success continues: In 1988, 1989 and again in 1990 we have scored
major military victories. We effectively control 90% of
the country. Unfortunately whenever we make peaceful
proposals they think we are suing for peace out of a
position of weakness. Ultimately this has been to their
cost.

"There is a serious possibility, if the situation
continues, that the next Ethiopian offensive will lead to
a major debacle in the Ethiopian army; a collapse of
morale leading to a military collapse or mass surrender
in various parts of Eritrea including the capital, Asmara.
The collapse of the Ethiopian army would lead to a
collapse of the Ethiopian state as we know it. I personally, and the EPLF officially, would hate to see this. We
are not interested in Ethiopia's disintegration because for
one thing this would mean—for an independent Eritrea—hundreds of thousands of refugees coming in and
adding a burden to an already war ravaged country
which wants to concentrate its energies on reconstruction. We could not refuse these refugees because we
ourselves know the meaning of being a refugee. That is

*In 1977 the EPLF controlled 90 percent of Eritrea when the Soviet
Union intervened on behalf of Ethiopia with massive military
supplies. The once prosperous highland town of Nacfa was completely
destroyed by Soviet-supplied bombers. In mid-1990 only two towns,
the capital, Asmara, and Keren, remain in Ethiopian hands.
Militarily capable of taking the towns, the EPLF knows that without
ground-to-air defenses the Ethiopian Air Force would destroy them.*

an elementary pragmatic view. Beyond that, Ethiopia as a nation deserves to be maintained. We have never wanted Ethiopia to be destroyed. However we want the Ethiopians to understand that we are determined to win our independence come what may."

The Responsibility of the Superpowers

"I would hope that the big powers, particularly the Soviet Union, which is the most influential power vis-à-vis the Ethiopian government, in view of the general spirit of disengagement which prevails, will use its influence to secure a political solution for Eritrea. In a major sense the superpowers have actually created our tragedy. The United States lined up political support for Ethiopian ambitions in Eritrea in the first place. In 1977-78 a switch of alliances took place when the Americans were thrown out of Ethiopia. When the Soviets arrived they changed from an earlier support for Eritrean independence—*independence* mind you—to support the Ethiopian effort to crush Eritrea. If there is no political solution then the answer to your question 'are we determined on a military victory': of course we are. What alternative do we have?

"Future historians may disagree, but in my opinion Eritrea's betrayal by the superpowers has steeled the Eritreans and made them even more determined. The creation of a sense of self-reliance, of not depending on

In March 1988 the EPLF broke out of its defensive lines and began a series of attacks designed to break Ethiopian military power in Eritrea and force Ethiopia to the negotiating table. Near the garrison town of Afabet they caught the retreating Ethiopian army.

The Ethiopian high command considered Afabet impregnable and did not prepare for the eventual destruction of the military supplies stored there which were captured by the EPLF in 1988.

At Afabet an EPLF fighter ignores an Ethiopian army signboard showing the medals and decorations which could be earned for valour and bravery.

outsiders, has become an important factor in our survival and helps explain our victories. The present climate of disengagement suggests that the Americans and Soviets are revising their earlier policies of blind support of their clients in the Horn. The growing realization that Ethiopia cannot achieve a military victory in Eritrea may convince them to rectify their past policy mistakes.

"The EPLF reminds the superpowers of their responsibility not only in the negative sense of what they have done to us but in a positive sense, as the leaders of the international community, to bring the Eritrean question to a peaceful end. Former President Jimmy Carter has attempted, with little success, to mediate in our talks with the Ethiopian government. The problem is that Mengistu's (the Ethiopian leader) career is based on his policy of a military solution in Eritrea. All of this tragedy; all these killings and destruction have been caused because of his insistence on a military solution. Ethiopians who have proposed a peaceful solution to the Eritrean situation have been summarily executed. The pressure for a peaceful solution threatens his survival. He is threatened not only in the professional sense, but his life is also at stake. So I think he—and those who are politically bound to him—will go right to the end unless he is overthrown. So there is a double obligation on the part of the superpowers; to recognize their past injustices and, in rectifying them, to create a framework—an international atmosphere—under which the Ethiopian government will have no choice but to deal politically.

"We are hopeful but sceptical. The USA and the Soviets have historically followed the same Greater Ethiopia Policy (which includes Eritrea) in the Horn of Africa and justified this policy with the same technical principles in international law which deny the moral and even the legal-historical basis of our argument; that we are a nation with every right—like other former colonies—

Since 1984 the EPLF has defeated Ethiopian forces in classic set tank and artillery battles. Captured tanks are repaired, cleaned and prepared for battle in EPLF workshops. **Next page:** Using Soviet supplied T-55 main battle tanks captured from the Ethiopian army an EPLF armored unit moves forward to new positions on the Nacfa Front.

to self-determination. Nevertheless they quote to us—or at us—what they call the Organization of African Unity principles that secession is counterproductive; fragmentation of nations is not helpful for economic as well as for other reasons. They say look at Biafra, look at Katanga and so on. That is why we feel that our historical and legal arguments, which are the basis of our case, are vital. We are *different* from Biafra or Katanga; we are more like Namibia, which has just received independence, and Western Sahara which is fighting against Moroccan imperialism. This difference is critical because it prevents false comparisons, fostered by years of Ethiopian propaganda, which claims we are secessionists. We are *not* interested in breaking up Ethiopia; but we are not Ethiopians, we are Eritreans. That is why we assert the historical basis of our claims for independence. If the international community and the Superpowers persist in resisting the legitimate demands for Eritrean independence *they* will be contributing to Ethiopia's breakup.

"Ultimately my ideal solution—something I dream to see before I die—is a group of independent nations, Ethiopia, Eritrea, Djibouti, Somalia, perhaps Sudan creating an economic common market in the Horn which could lead to a political union of some kind and which could be a model for the rest of Africa. This is a region with some of the most talented people in Africa, with resources sufficient to go around not only for their own populations but also outside the region. We want cohesion and stability not disintegration. But being coerced into a forced marriage with Ethiopia *is* a form of disintegration. It has led to the disintegration of our culture and dispersal of our people. We are three and half million people, with substantial resource endowments. We want what every nation has fought for: self-determination!"

A captured "Stalin Organ"—the rocket launcher's fearsome firepower is now turned on Ethiopian positions.

In 1990 the EPLF was holding approximately 50,000 prisoners of war, including Soviet adviser-officers. "We have no quarrel with them personally; they were conscripted, lied to, badly trained and sent to kill us. Even so we treat them humanely and give them a basic education—something they won't receive in Ethiopia. But it is a terrible burden for us to do this. The international aid community has been very slow in recognizing this problem because the Ethiopian government refuses to admit we have so many prisoners even though many journalists have seen them. Can you imagine how difficult it is for us to provide food, medical care and especially firewood for this many people under these conditions?" **Right:** The war has already lasted a generation; these Ethiopian POWs ponder how long they will have to wait to return home.

*"We have survived war for
a generation; if necessary
we will fight for another generation
but what we want
is peace."*

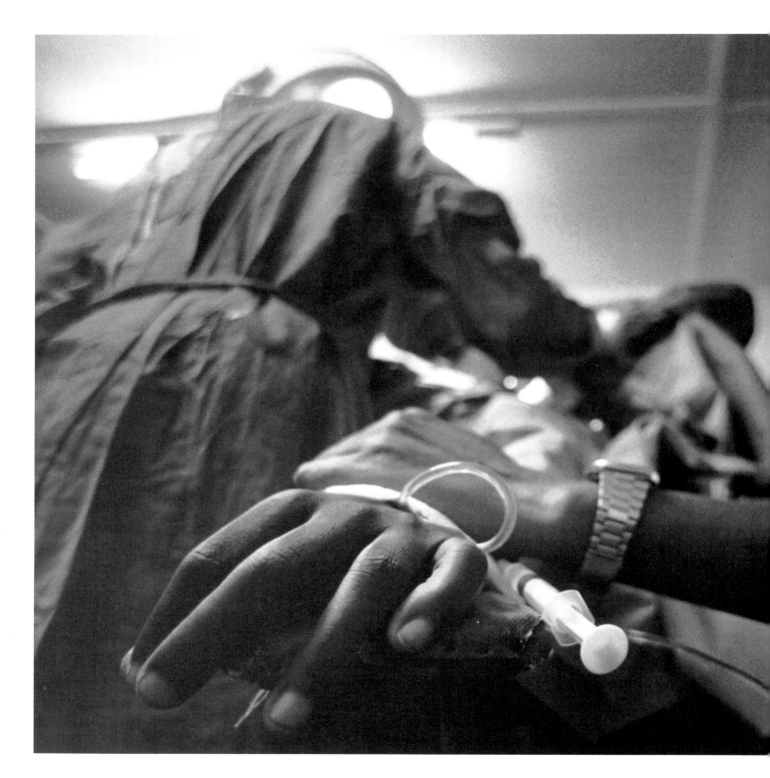

*Fighters know that when wounded the efficiency of the
Eritrean medical system gives them better than an 80
percent chance of survival.*

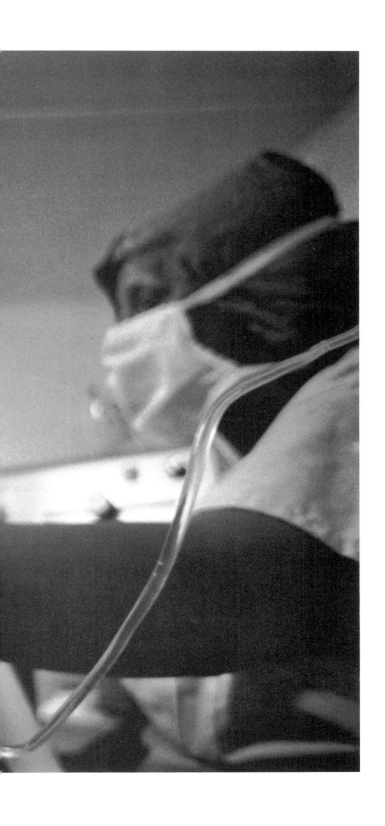

THE PRICE

"The screaming started at 4:00 A.M. It wasn't a scream of pain; it was a fighter's nightmare, reliving the destruction of his body."

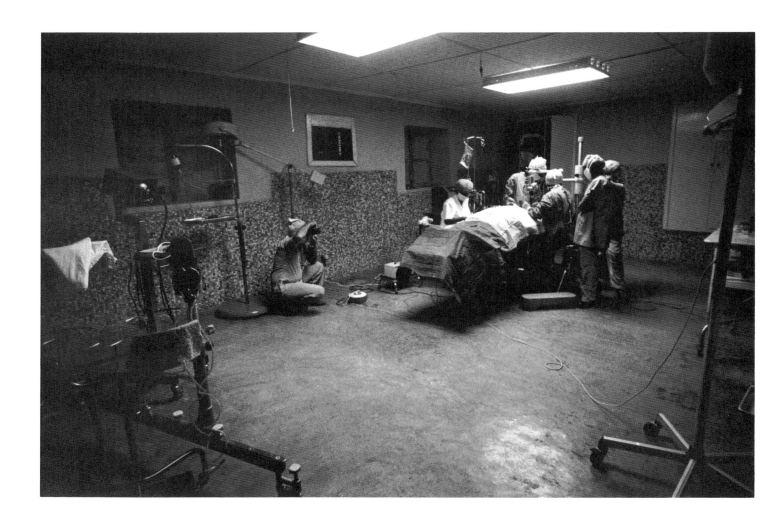

Dug into the hillsides of Orota a surgeon is photographed as he labors through the night repairing war damaged ears using microsurgery techniques. **Next Page:** *A generation of war has cost thousands of lives and deforming injuries.*

It is late afternoon at the EPLF Rehabilitation Hospital in Port Sudan where severely war injured are sent for rehabilitation, physiotherapy and continuing education. The hospital is a administered by former patients; the teachers often patients themselves. Here the physical price of the struggle is most evident; individual optimism most incongruous. Outside, camels graze among the wind blown refuse—the leavings of the poorest of the poor in one of the poorest countries in the world. Into this heat, dust and trash, in a clearing amidst barren concrete buildings protected by glass-topped walls and iron doors, war shattered fighters emerge to exercise— most of them land mine amputees, or spinal injured, struggling to convert their shuffles into a semblance of a walk, learning to live with the damage.

Nearby, Mebrat climbs into "her" Toyota Land Cruiser and wheels it around to be filled with fuel in the EPLF garage prior to starting the long drive into Eritrea. She discusses the car's condition with the mechanics and makes them rock the sturdy four-wheel drive while it is

filled with gasoline to ensure that the tanks take the full measure she has been allotted. She needs eleven layers of quilt on the seat to reach the pedals; her diminutive size, youthful face and fastidiously neat dress—home tailored tight fitting trousers and shirt with brown V-neck sweater—mask a tough professional driver who spent years in the front lines. A passenger who carelessly flicks cigarette ashes on the floor of her neatly swept Toyota only does this once.

Desert Moonscape

The EPLF garage is an oil-soaked desert moonscape dotted with old shipping containers converted into sleeping rooms where mechanics work around the clock to the dull knocking of diesel generators and the eerie white-green light of a forest of bare fluorescent lamps. The garage is capable of rebuilding any truck from top to bottom and is the beginning of the lifeline between Sudan and Eritrea. The mechanics and drivers are the unremarked heroes of the Eritrean struggle and certainly of emergency food aid efforts; they keep the supply

lifeline flowing. Without them everything withers and dies within weeks.

We start the punishing trip into Eritrea in 104-degree afternoon heat on an asphalt road which breaks up into a sandy washboard after a few miles and which we soon abandon for one of the tracks in the desert. The remnants of the road and the shreds of wire hanging from the telegraph poles attest to an earlier prosperous and peaceful trade between Sudan and Eritrea; a trade which has been largely replaced by convoys of aid trucks carry food to feed the hundreds of thousands of refugees created by the war. For hours we bump across the desert; how Mebrat finds the way is her secret, especially after dark. Having left any Sudanese presence hours behind us we arrive at the Eritrean "border" at dusk. Armed fighters of the EPLA welcome us to Eritrea. Our names are logged into an arrival book, our "visas"—letters of authorization issued in Khartoum—are checked and Mebrat registers the car with its freight, cold boxes full of vaccines and miscellaneous spare parts. Transportation is precious and in addition to the supplies nine passengers crowd the Land Cruiser. We are

At an EPLF hospital in Sudan EPLF fighters undergo rehabilitation designed to minimize their injuries and reintegrate them quickly back into Eritrean society. **Below:** For quadraplegics, bed is a prison from which they will never be released. **Next Page:** At the Solomuna Orphanage a fighter turned psychologist teaches himself to understand the problems of the children.

forced to travel at night because during the day predatory Ethiopian Migs can appear at any moment, cruising slowly at low altitudes seeking targets for their loads of cluster bombs and napalm. The lack of ground to air defenses has turned Eritrean society inside out; only with the safety of dusk does the revolution comes to life—generators are started, workshops begin to produce everthing from sandals to sophisticated pharmaceuticals to replacement gun stocks. At first light everything will stop, suspended, waiting again for darkness.

Earlier we had passed an Eritrean Relief Association (ERA) food convoy crawling at 10 miles per hour as it approached a river swollen by flash floods where the seven-ton trucks would be pulled across, one by one, by a mammoth six-wheel-drive Russian Zil truck, captured from the Ethiopian army. It was hard to believe heavy trucks can make this journey at all. The secret is speed—or lack of it. "A truck can last a long time and go just about anywhere—*if* you take care of it and drive slowly enough." one of the drivers explained. In the next weeks I would have ample proof of this, watching ERA trucks creep through steep canyons and along boulder strewn

dry river beds. A network of service and repair stations equipped with simple, often self-made machinery, camouflaged under acacia trees or dug into hillsides, keep the trucks moving. Mebrat, like the other drivers, ends her day by checking the oil and cleaning the air filters. She keeps a full mechanical record of the car in the glove compartment, which also contains all of her personal belongings.

POWs

From the blackness of a moonless night shapes begin to emerge in the first grey half-light of morning; we are driving along the bottom of a narrow canyon. The shadowy light plays tricks with our eyes—the sides of the canyon seem to undulate—and it is few minutes before I realize that this apparition is actually the movement of thousands of waking Ethiopian prisoners of war. In 1985 the EPLF claimed to hold 8,000 POWS; by 1988 journalists reports supported their claim of 20,000 and this has more than doubled during 1990. Because the Ethiopian government denies the existence of the

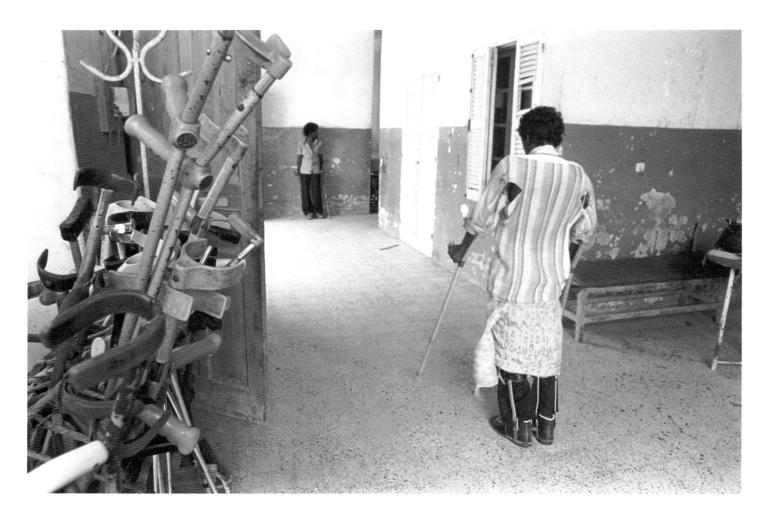

war, the International Red Cross was unable or unwilling to offer POW aid until recently when the number of prisoners could no longer be ignored or denied.

We stop for the day at the camp, waiting for the night. We unintentionally offend our hosts by declining to interview prisoners. We feel they are too vulnerable to speak freely; our hosts take pride in the EPLF's humane treatment of the POWS, most of whom are illiterate peasant conscripts. EPLF officials take us on a tour of the camp—there is no barbed wire and little evidence of guards, mostly because there is no place to run. We see obviously well fed prisoners building shelters, attending school and playing football. Officials explain that all POWs are required to attend school where they learn basic literacy, history and the origins of the war which have brought them to this place.

Tragically, after a generation of war, Ethiopia, the poorest country in Africa, with the third largest standing army and a decade of massive military debts to the Soviet Union and its former East European client states, continues to seek a military solution in Eritrea. Two-thirds of Ethiopia's 350,000-man army is stationed in

Eritrea. An estimated 250,000 soldiers have died on the battlefields. During the 1984-85 famine 45 percent of Ethiopia's budget was devoted to security and defense, most of this to continue the war in Eritrea. The costs of failing to achieve political settlements effectively pre-empts meaningful economic development within Ethiopia itself and severely limits improvements in the whole of the Horn of Africa.

More than a million Eritreans has been forced to become refugees or displaced persons within Eritrea. While the EPLF can be rightly proud of its achievements in education, medical care and self reliant economic development, until peace is achieved the full potential of Eritrea's people remains locked in the repetitive waste of war. The lives of everyone in Eritrea—and in Ethiopia—are distorted and diminished by the war and the terrible price it demands.

Chuchu

Chuchu is a guide at the EPLF Rest House in Orota. She takes visitors—mostly journalists, members of sup-

The fear of Ethiopian Mig-23s demands that travel takes place only after dark. Precious fuel is scrupulously accounted for; each driver responsible for efficient fuel usage and the mechanical maintenance of their vehicle.

port groups, and representatives of political or aid and development organizations—through the EPLF-controlled areas of Eritrea. However startling it is for visitors to discover, in what appears to be an uninhabited canyon, an underground workshop making women's sanitary towels, Chuchu has been there hundreds of times answering the same questions. Attractive, stylish—even in a field jacket—ironic, she charms everyone, especially the photographers. In her mid-thirties, she married two years ago but sees her husband infrequently—he works elsewhere in the Orota base area. Chuchu lives in one small room and everything she owns packs into a little canvas bag. Like all members of the EPLF she receives no salary. She has committed her life to the struggle for independence—everything else has to wait: she is a fighter.

"I was born near the Ethiopia-Kenya border, a rich, fertile place. We have five kinds of potatoes and many kinds of fruit, wild bananas and wild coffee. Sometimes when walking in the forest the trees are so thick you can't see the sun. I really liked that place and only left to continue my education in Addis Ababa.

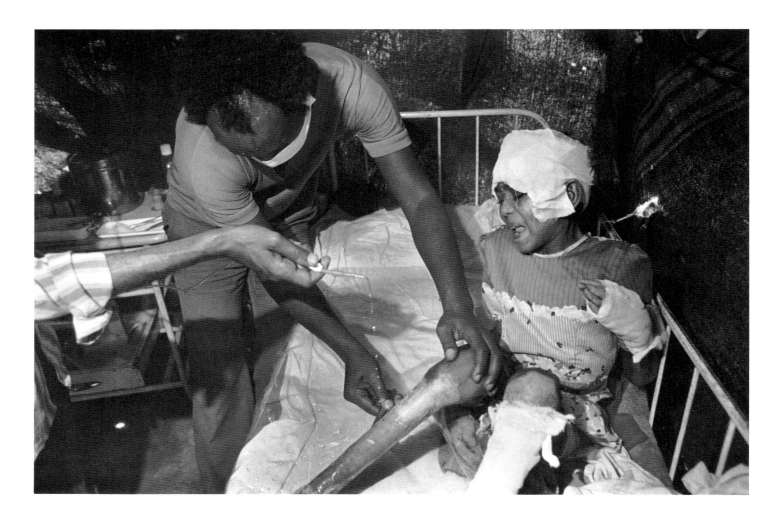

Terhas' father carried her for days to reach an EPLF hospital after an Ethiopian napalm attack. Isolated against infection in a "room" made from recycled food aid bags, her bandages are changed twice each day. The pain is excruciating; her scream unheard—Terhas never makes a sound.

"Even though we lived in Ethiopia my father taught us to be proud to be Eritrean. He worked as a dresser preparing bandages at the clinic. He used to tell us that *we* should choose what we want to do and be. Although he earned a very small salary each month he educated all of us, even the girls. We weren't very sophisticated—we lived very simply. We had enough to eat but that was all. When an elder brother got a book he took care of it so I could have it later. So I only had to buy exercise books. My mother couldn't see the use of education but my father supported it.

"I first went to Addis Ababa on the bus. We had to walk six or seven hours to get to the place where we could catch the bus. When I arrived in Addis I had never seen a city before—my home had 50,000 people but we had no electricity or running water. What I remember most about Addis were all the cars—but the rest didn't impress me much. The life of young people seemed senseless and foolish to me. Many of the young people from my town wanted very much to come to Addis and stay but when school finished on the 29th of June—on the 30th I was on the bus returning home.

"When I was a child, when my father asked me what I wanted to become, I told him 'a traveller—with a small green tent and a small green cup.' My first night with the EPLF they gave me a place to sleep in a green tent—I couldn't believe it. And I have a small cup in my bag. And now I am a traveller, guiding visitors in Eritrea. I never thought I would live ten years after becoming a fighter but somehow I have survived. I have learned to accept reality—whether it is right or wrong."

"Accepting reality" is Chuchu's way of explaining that her father and elder brother were murdered by the Ethiopian army for supporting the EPLF. Virtually every Eritrean family has a similar story to tell; everyone has been directly affected by the war and the particular brutality of the Ethiopian military and security forces. Chuchu's situation is unusual in the sense that after independence she will have no place in Eritrea to return to; her struggle is more abstract—it is for the ideal of Eritrea.

"Sometimes well meaning visitors come here and tell us how good it is that we live so simply, sitting on small stools, living in little rooms made of stone, having

The Ethiopian army has buried tens of thousands of land mines. Nomad shepherds, mostly children, are their most common victim. After the war ends it will take years, if not decades, to clear Eritrea of these mutilators.

little and writing all of our lessons in one exercise book. But we don't want this—circumstances force us to live like this—we want chairs and proper houses and an exercise book for each lesson. We are fighting for that but many visitors find our simplicity romantic. They are attracted—some even say this directly—by our sense of purpose and self-sacrifice but they don't realize how difficult it is to live like this year after year."

Terror against Civilians

In 1988 the war became even more brutal. The EPLF broke out of the defensive positions it had held for a decade and began a series of spectacular offensives meant to force the Ethiopians to the negotiating table or, failing that, to outright defeat of the Ethiopian army in the field. The audacious initiative of the EPLF, whose forces are estimated at 35,000—less than one-tenth of Ethiopia's—started in the spring of 1988 when the EPLF captured the "unconquerable" garrison town of Afabet and destroyed an entire Ethiopian Division. Within nine months they had surrounded the key town of Keren, had sunk the better part of the Ethiopian navy in the Red Sea, were fighting for control of the port of Massawa and were poised to attack the capital of Eritrea,

Asmara. The Dergue responded with a campaign of terror against civilians, declaring entire areas—especially the fertile and densely populated coastal regions—free fire zones, intending to burden the EPLF with even more refugees while attempting to physically destroy their political base in the countryside. Hundreds of thousands of productive farmers were converted into aid-dependent refugees. In 1990 the failure of the rains in marginal areas plus the loss of food production in relatively fertile areas led to a famine which in many ways was worse than that of 1984-85. Mohammed Amin, the cameraman whose film of the 1984 famine shown on the BBC had shocked the world, claimed that famine in neighboring Tigre was worse in 1990 than in anything he had seen in 1984. The story of this largely man-made famine was reported in the media to an "aided-out" public consumed by the dramatic changes taking place in the Soviet Union, eastern Europe, and South Africa. Eritrea and Tigray—the two objects of Ethiopia's scorched earth policy—became the epicenters of the 1990 famine.

In late summer 1988 I met Amena at Rora Nacfa, a new refugee settlement in the highlands near the hundreds of miles of trenches which had divided Eritrean and Ethiopian fighters for a decade. Everywhere newly arrived refugees were struggling to build shelter.

A land mine victim recovers at the EPLF rehabilitation center at Suakin, Sudan—her handmade bedding a gift from Eritrean refugees living abroad.

Dr. Assafaw, the head of the civilian hospital, with a napalm scarred child.

Amena and her daughter Adema, age 2, were living in a stick and branch hut: they had just survived the massacre at She'eb, where 400 villagers were murdered by Ethiopian troops. "Anything you gave to our land at She'eb—it would grow—sorghum, millet, sesame, watermelons, tomatoes, vegetables. On May 12 two tanks with soldiers arrived. They told the people not to run away. There were only old people, children and women there because the men know that when the Ethiopians come they will be conscripted or arrested and so they had already fled.

"Once we were gathered the soldiers started shooting the people with the machine gun on the tank and the other tank drove into the crowd crushing people. I was lucky, there was a tree nearby and I managed to get behind it and the bodies of the murdered fell on me and my child. My son Idris and my daughter Fatma were killed along with my mother, two sisters and my sister-in-law.

"The soldiers went through the bodies killing those who were still alive and looting, taking the jewelry. I was covered with blood and when the came to me I pretended to be dead. But even though I had covered my Adema with bloody clothes they discovered her because she was crying. One soldier said 'kill her' but the other said it wasn't necessary—she will die of thirst anyway. Then the soldiers began to kill the animals—it was so stupid, they couldn't even eat all of them. Then they burned the houses and destroyed the ovens for nothing.

"The soldier stayed in the village for three days. I had to lay among the bodies with my child during that time. It was too dangerous to try to leave. On the third night the soldiers left and I managed to run away after dark. We walked all night. When the sun came up we waited under trees afraid of the Migs. When we reached a place called Inn we found the fighters. An EPLF Mobile Medical Unit gave us medical help and arranged for us to be taken by truck to Afabet. We arrived in Afabet on the 16th of May. The Amharas [Ethiopians] are killing many civilians now. They can't stand up to the EPLF fighters and so they kill us."

"I was cultivating one morning when the Migs came . . . "

As we spoke with some of the survivors of the war wrecked town of Afabet in the summer of 1988 Abdu Ali, 64, approached us demanding to be heard:

"I was at She'eb when the Ethiopians came. They began killing everyone. My mother was killed when they crushed us with tanks. I watched people purposely blinded and left. They didn't waste many bullets on us—they used the bayonets."

As he speaks a passerby seeing us taking notes and shouts: "These people are writing but it won't help you!" Our critic's comment is difficult to dispute in Eritrea. Journalists and scholars have written about Eritrea's plight for a generation but the war goes on, largely ignored by the international community and by the United Nations and the Organization of African Unity, the only bodies with the political influence to negotiate a political resolution. Eritreans pay this terrible price because their experience had taught them that only by depending on themselves will Eritrea ever be independent.

Practicing outmoded agricultural techniques, with little incentive to improve their land, highland farmers stoically faced years of drought which cumulated in the famine of 1984-85.

FAMINE

*In 1984-1985
and again in 1990,
a decade of drought
and a generation of war
threatened the lives
of millions.*

Although Eritrea was at the epicenter of the 1984-85 famine and the Eritrean Relief Association (ERA) had an international reputation for honesty and efficiency, Eritrea received little aid. With one son dead, and another dying, this mother, crushed with grief, mourns together with her relatives, themselves hardly more than skeletons.

Nomadic societies were particularly hard hit by the famine. Widely scattered, they could not be easily reached and ERA had to wait for them to arrive at aid stations. After weeks of travel, this family arrived to late to save their son.

What became known as the Ethiopian famine of 1984-85 had, in reality, raged for more than a year before it became an international news story. Because the international community regards Eritrea as an integral part of Ethiopia and the EPLF as a secessionist movement, Western aid officials estimate that Eritrea received less than 5 percent of the international aid donated to relieve hunger and save lives.

The Famine in Erota

At Erota in the Eritrean highlands, Ibraham, the head of the new Village Assembly, explains how the famine developed. "In Erota, inadequate rain had fallen in eight of the fourteen years since 1970. The poverty of our area developed over years as we experienced year after year of drought. By 1983-84 it was very bad. In 1984 it did not rain at all and the agricultural system collapsed but by this time people were already very poor and had no reserves, either in food or money, and people began to

Even though the EPLF effectively administers 90 percent of Eritrea, famine aid for Eritrea was given to Ethiopia. The Ethiopian army used food in their fight against the EPLF, refused to distribute to suspected "sympathizers," or sold large quantities of donated food, like the bags pictured here, to Sudanese traders.

leave for Sudan or for the Gash River, a more fertile area which does not depend on rain.

"A family of five needs at least twelve sacks of durrah [a form of sorghum] to survive properly; we had been getting only three and in 1984 we got almost nothing. Old people stopped eating—their contribution to saving the young. They were often too old to travel and they preferred to die in their homes. Families had to decide which of the children to feed and which would die.

"In 1985 it was a little better and then bad again in 1986. The price of grain kept going up and the price of animals went down to the point where one could buy a cow for one bag of durrah but there was nothing to feed it. The owners of livestock were hurt most. People who had sixty goats were left with five or six. The cattle keepers left entirely—they would have lost all of their animals if they had stayed. They tried to get to the Gash River area—about a two-week walk—but many didn't make it."

By 1990, the small gains made in the previous years were wiped out by an almost total failure of the rains.

"Ten thousand people lived here before the drought, 7,000 have returned. This was once a prosperous place but now after years of drought it is very poor. People can only stay here because ERA brings food in return for work. The work we do is reforestation, terracing, land improvement, the new poultry project and, of course, community organization. The drought is not our only problem; the war has distorted everything. We cannot plough and plant in the normal way because we are afraid of the Migs. Many people have given up cultivating because they fear the planes and they know their fields will reveal where they are living."

Yosief, my guide and interpreter, a former attorney in Addis, adds, "One of the reasons for the famine was that the Ethiopian government conscripted too many farmers for the 1982 and 1983 offensives leaving land unplanted or poorly planted and tended. Everywhere in Eritrea the Ethiopians have indiscriminately planted land mines to discourage farmers from planting, turning thousands of productive farmers into refugees."

Ibraham continues, "ERA wants us to plan for the long term but how can we do that when we don't know if we will be able to stay in this place? We can only stay here now because of ERA which provides the food we can't grow. When we get extras like milk powder and sugar, we give the milk to pregnant women and children. It is the same for our new poultry project—the eggs are given to those who need this food most. We decide this as a community in our Village Assembly; each person and each department is accountable to the village."

Eritrean Relief Association

It is 1985 but the imagery is biblical: heavily laden camel caravans emerge out of the heat waves of the desert but they are not carrying frankincense and myrrh. Their load is U.S.-donated food aid bought from Ethiopian military officials. They stop for the night at Germaika, a new trading center grown up in the desert to provide for the caravans trading food aid between Ethiopia and Sudan. Reluctantly, Ali, a trader, explains: "I pay 300 Sudanese pounds per 100 kg for milk powder from the Ethiopians; I sell in Sudan for 500 pounds. This trip I am taking 2400 kg. I've made many journeys already. Could I buy twice or three times as much? Of course! All I need is the money."

Tekie, an ERA senior official, sits slouched on a mud brick bed covered with hand made patchwork quilts in the sweltering heat of our tent in Himbol, the

In 1984-85 the Eritrean-staffed Eritrean Relief Association (ERA) planned and carried out what Western senior aid workers described as "the most effective emergency aid program in the Sahel." Lives were needlessly lost because ERA simply could not get enough donated food to distribute. ERA trucks loaded with food are camouflaged during the day in mountain valleys too narrow for the Ethiopian Migs. At dusk the drivers will continue the slow, tortuous journey into the famine areas: 125 miles will take nearly fourteen hours. Next Page: Without ERA this mother and child would have died.

center of ERA operations within Eritrea. His second-hand clothes hang on his bony frame; his shirt pocket jammed with bits of paper, each with an urgent message. He smiles easily, speaks quickly and with great passion; a man under pressure: he is responsible for thirty-one camps crowded with famine refugees.

"ERA is an independent volunteer organization. We work with the EPLF. Like every organization in Eritrea, military or civilian, no one is paid—not one cent. We receive a place to sleep and our food and the clothes we wear. It is not because we want it this way; we simply don't have enough money to pay salaries.

"The head office of ERA is in Khartoum. We also have offices in Europe, the Middle East and North America. We operate in areas we fully control but we also function behind the lines in the semiliberated areas. We provide emergency help and we help people to help themselves by helping to plan development projects and by giving organizational aid to the Village Assemblies.

"We have had to establish thirty-one emergency feeding camps which housed about 110,000 people and we had to temporarily bring another 100,000 people to Sudan. But our basic philosophy is to keep people home and to bring food and services to them and eventually to train local people to improve their community and make them less vulnerable to drought. People are dying in Eritrea because of the famine but we are able to do a lot and the fighters are giving 150 grams of their 500 gram ration to the civilians and this is saving many lives.

"In the past Eritrean agriculture was self-sufficient; Italy *exported* food from Eritrea; now at least one-third of the population is dependent on food aid. The drought dramatically affected production in certain areas but with proper distribution famine could have been prevented. It is the war which creates famine."

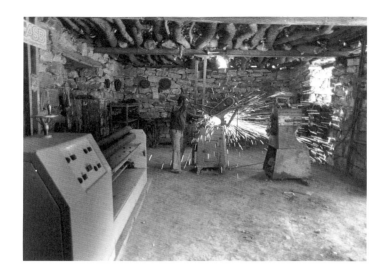

In 1989-90 more than 80 percent of the crop failed in Eritrea, Tigray and parts of Ethiopia: nearly 2 million people are again at risk. ERA's success depends on the efficiency of its staff, the availability of food and its ability to maintain a transportation lifeline— trucks. The life of aid trucks is normally measured in months. ERA's trucks, maintained in their own underground workshops by Eritreans, is measured in years.

Emergency aid is life saving but does not alter the conditions which favor famine. At Agraa ERA created a vast, irrigated agricultural scheme. "In the long term it is a mistake," I was told by an ERA official, "because it was too expensive and relies on mechanization local people cannot sustain. We can't afford such capital intensive projects. But it did save lives because we produced a great deal of food quickly."

At the Solomuna Camp inside Eritrea a frightened child takes refuge inside the bomb shelter which each family must build.

REFUGEES

*"A generation of war
has forced a third
of our population
to live
as refugees."*

Solomuna inhabitants are mostly women and children with an uncertain future; many have lived here a decade. The camp is an example of the social transformations which the EPLF is attempting to make. ERA provides resources, the women themselves administer the camp, distribute and account for food.

As Balkan Airlines begins its descent into Amsterdam's Schipol Airport, two Eritrean passengers, Wolde, a former teacher in his mid-twenties, and his pregnant wife Saba, begin to tear up their United Nations Travel Documents, air tickets, personal identity papers and nearly $1000 in travellers checks—all to be flushed down the toilet. They intend to seek political asylum in Holland. If the Dutch immigration officials can prove their place of origin they are required to send them back. Saba, who speaks only Tigrinya, is two months from delivering her child who she hopes will be born on Dutch soil. They will stay hours in the transit lounge until it is no longer possible to identify their incoming flight, then they will apply for asylum and begin a long, nerve-wracking months-long wait while their application is processed.

Their arrival in Amsterdam is only the last part of a desperate journey which began six months earlier. It was forced by a surprise Ethiopian raid in the town of

Keren seeking EPLF sympathizers, an escape into the night, weeks of travel, an illegal entry into Sudan followed by five months of hiding in Khartoum while trying to obtain travel documents and money to flee and then hours of detention and interrogation during an overnight stopover in pro-Ethiopian Bulgaria. At different times and in different ways hundreds of thousands of Eritreans have made similar journeys into exile.

Eritrea has the largest proportion of refugees of any country in Africa: nearly one-third of its 3.5 million people. Most of the refugees within and outside of Eritrea are the result of political persecution and war; not famine. While the EPLF seeks to offer refugees accommodation within Eritrea, limited resources, lack of work and the fear of war force 600,000 Eritreans to live in appalling conditions in camps in Sudan while a further 500,000 are scattered throughout Europe, the Middle East and North America. Their number grows each day.

The continuation of the war and the creation of refugees in the Horn of Africa has been a major factor in the development of famine. Material and human

resources are restricted to refugee camps instead of improving the agricultural infrastructures which could reduce vulnerability to famine.

Solomuna Camp

Solomuna Camp is the oldest and most developed of the refugee settlements. It is a concrete example of how EPLF policies of self reliance, self government and social change are implemented.

"The camp started in 1975," my guide Chuchu explains, "because of the growing number of women refugees as more and more men were imprisoned or massacred as the Dergue sought to kill or imprison any opposition, and women found themselves destitute— widows with small children. Many would have been forced into prostitution to survive but the EPLF created this alternative. In 1981, after the Orota base area was considered secure the camp was moved to its present location here in the mountains at Solomuna.

"In 1982 the first People's Assembly was created to allow camp residents to learn to govern themselves. It

took 6-8 years to evolve into the present self-governing structure. The women administer the camp and evaluate their food needs—as you can see it is not possible to grow food here due to lack of arable land, water and security problems—and then present them to ERA. When the food arrives the camp members are in charge of distribution and accounting. The sense of community is so strong that even during the famine food could be left unguarded, stored under trees and was not stolen. Administration is entirely in the hands of women, no outside officials supervise it. But the women are required to account to ERA for all foods and materials received.

"New arrivals are accommodated by the People's Assembly. Most of them have lost everything. The workshops in the camp provide the basic utensils for a household. It is our tradition in the EPLF to make do with what we have. When we don't have shirts we don't complain, we make them from what we can find—old food bags or whatever.

"The camp is also innovative. It has a bakery which produces for everyone using electric ovens donated by Eritreans abroad. Because fire wood is so scarce it is better to bake using electricity from diesel generators. We are very concerned about deforestation and conserving wood is a major priority. *Njera*, our traditional bread, is also made in one of the communal kitchens—another attempt to save wood by reducing the number of cooking fires. After dusk when it is safe, water is brought by tanker trucks and distributed from holding tanks. The camp has simple health facilities and an extensive child and adult education system; the majority of women here are attending school at some level. There is also a new poultry project. For many women, chickens and eggs were unknown before coming here.

"Many of the women have lived in the camp for more than a decade. One of the most important long-term effects on the residents is the self confidence and new image which women acquire. They take responsibil-ity for their lives and the lives of their colleagues. Ask them. They will tell you!"

Adu lives in a one-room house made of recycled food sacks sewn together. The roof, like all roofs in the settlement, is camouflaged with shrubs. Her furniture is made of mud and stones, her bed a mud brick platform covered with striking patchwork quilts made by the women. It is life at the material minimum but she speaks with a tremendous enthusiasm. Her story is told over and over by the women of Solomuna.

"It was a hard time under the colonizers [Ethiopians]. We lived in Asmara but my family comes from a nearby village. I was engaged at eight and married at twelve to a man I had never seen before. My husband was a carpenter but he couldn't always find work and we were very poor. In 1975 we left Asmara and returned to the village.

"In 1978 the Ethiopians started killing people. Our village was burned because we were suspected of sup-

*In order to save scarce firewood, cooking and baking are done in central kitchens. **Below:** Workers at the orphanage prepare a special protein rich spaghetti which contains DMK, a locally produced food supplement. **Next Page:** Water, also in short supply, must be trucked to the camp and distributed at dusk when the danger of air attack is minimal.*

porting the EPLF. They killed my husband and stoned my mother-in-law to death. I have six children; three are fighters, two boys and a girl and three are with me here—two in the boarding school and one still lives with me here in Solomuna.

"When I arrived here I had lived a completely traditional life. I was totally dependent on my husband and when he was killed I had nothing. Now I can read and write and I have enough to eat. You don't know what it means not to have to worry about getting enough to eat. But most important to me; I have the right to *say* what I want—this was unthinkable before. In the old way I had to suppress my thoughts about daily problems, the family, financial problems, political ideas—I couldn't say anything. I accepted a totally dependent role—even within my own house. If I complained or spoke out I was beaten. I was given a small part of my husband's money each month and was expected to care for the entire family. Usually it wasn't

enough even when I was very careful. Often we were hungry and there was nothing I could do.

"Now I feel free. I have the right to speak and to criticize and to develop myself through learning. I was completely uneducated when I arrived here; now I am in grade four! I never thought at age forty-two I could learn to read and write. Now that I am literate I am learning to be a TBA—traditional birth attendant. I could never dream of such a thing before.

"I don't want to stay here forever; I want to go home. But I will go home a completely different person than when I left. I will know something and be able to help others."

Free-Fire Zones

Since 1988 Ethiopia's military strategy in Eritrea has centered on creating refugees through terror against civilians as a way of breaking EPLF support in the countryside and forcing the EPLF to commit its limited

resources to refugee settlement. Aside from the human misery this has created it was also a major cause of the 1990 famine. In the spring of 1988 Ethiopian troops, mechanized units and aircraft began a series of attacks on civilian populations especially along the fertile eastern coastal lands, declaring large areas free fire-zones, and driving thousands of self-sufficient farmers into refugee camps. The most notorious of these attacks was on the village of She'eb. ERA officials, whose research department provides highly accurate information of population movements and agricultural production, were predicting that famine would follow in 1989-90. As Lilo, the senior ERA official inside Eritrea told me, "The next famine will be almost entirely man-made." The rains failed in 1989-1990 but for tens of thousands of Eritrean farmers it hardly mattered; they had fled their farms months before and were already living on donated food in refugee settlements. The farmers most able to produce the surpluses which could have fended off famine were

now themselves the recipients of food aid, driven out of their homes by the terror.

Rora Nacfa is a new refugee settlement of one room "houses" dug into the hillsides, strung for miles along a steep, stony canyon near the destroyed town of Nacfa. By mid-August, 8,700 refugees had arrived— throughout the summer and fall new refugees continued to flee the Ethiopian terror. Many of the newly arrived refugees believe the Ethiopians are seeking a "Final Solution" intending to either kill or drive out the entire Eritrean population and take their land.

Tzeghannes, 53, a former village headman, greets us with his left hand—the right has been shredded by shrapnel.

"It was early in the morning, the older children had already gone out to the fields. When they started bombing we ran with the children who were with us: we don't know what has happened to the others. In the chaos we had to leave three children behind. The Der-

gue doesn't differentiate between civilians and fighters, they destroy everything.

"Our village is now ashes, destroyed by aerial bombardment and the canons. Many people were killed and wounded. Many families have been broken up—not everyone could escape. We left behind everything: we had nothing when we arrived here."

Ashgedom, 42, who is sitting nearby, can contain himself no longer and interrupts, "Yes, it was early in the morning when the Ethiopians came. The animals were still in the compound. We didn't know what to do so we just opened the gate and let them go. We ran out of the house and kept running.

"Here we can't produce anything because there is no land and no water and we have no animals. We depend on food hand-outs. But we try to organize ourselves to help build houses for new arrivals, especially for women who are arriving without husbands and who have small children.

"We left during the harvest season. We had worked for a year. We had cut the crops but didn't have time to thresh the plants. The coffee beans were still on the plants. We had to leave it all. In 1984-85, during the drought, we had very little rain and people had a hard time but after that this area returned to what it was— very fertile. We grow barley, wheat, maize, potatoes, tomatoes, coffee. Coffee is the cash crop.

"Twice a year the Ethiopian soldiers came—but only for a day—ours is an EPLF semi-liberated area which means that the Ethiopians are afraid to stay overnight. We used to take all of our belongings out of the village and hide them. When they came they would loot and break our water jugs, shoot jerry cans, break the clay ovens—just childish things but they cost us much trouble.

"The Ethiopians *know* that the Eritreans are not pro-Ethiopian—we never were. What they want is our land. They don't care about us as a people—their aim is to exterminate us and take our land. They don't trust the Eritreans. They can never win our trust. How could they, the way they treat us?

"Our aim is to go back to our villages. We know the EPLF will win. When the enemy is pushed out we will return but only when they are gone. We are optimistic. Everybody is a supporter of the EPLF because they know that the EPLF will bring independence. We have our children in the EPLF: my daughter is a fighter."

Tzeghannes describes what has happened to agriculture in his area, one of the most fertile in Eritrea.

"Our main village of Wokizager in the highlands is about six hours walk from Asmara. But now it takes more than a day because of the detours necessary to avoid the land mines and the harassment from the

security checkpoints. Often they dump our grain on the road searching for grenades and we have to repack it. When we walked to our second farm at Faghena on the escarpment it used to take two hours but now it takes about ten hours due to the detours and the checkpoints along the road. It is very dangerous. Many people have been killed by land mines as have many, many cattle.

"In the highlands the main rains fall October to April. In August we start to prepare the land, sowing takes place in October and in March-May we harvest. The coffee harvest is gradual, not all at once. After the harvests there is not much work and we used this time to improve the fields and to manure them.

"On the escarpment the rains fall in July-August. Therefore it is possible to harvest twice: once in the highlands and once on the escarpment. We used to live in Wokizager which was our main farming area (Faghena was always 'extra' land) in the highlands. But the highlands became too dangerous since the Ethiopians regarded highlanders as EPLF supporters and frequently destroyed their villages. We were afraid to travel from the highlands to the escarpment so we stayed on the escarpment—not because we preferred it but it was safer.

"When we had both the highland and escarpment farms were could harvest a minimum of twenty quintals [4,440 lbs] but now with only the escarpment we are lucky to get 5 quintals [1100 lbs]. We only stay in the

When asked why they stay in Eritrea, enduring the constant danger of air attack, women answer: "This is our home; here we have a future; we are going to school; we decide how the camp is operated. If we go to Sudan it is safer but we have nothing to do; no future, no education."

escarpment because of fear; everyone prefers the high-lands.

"Even in Faghena we can't farm properly. We are 'visited' occasionally [by troops] and bombardments take place. Five quintals for a family of 4-7 lasts only three months. We tried collecting firewood to sell and we began to gather wild fruits and vegetables to eat. Life was very hard. There were three types of peasants in the past: rich ones who harvested 30-50 quintals per year, middle peasants who got 15-25 and the poor who got fifteen or less. Now everyone is a poor peasant.

"In the 1970s we harvested forty quintals of pota-toes, fifteen quintals of wheat and five quintals of beans. We were rich peasants. The 1972-73 famine was bad but not so severe for us because we could farm freely. By working hard we could overcome it even though we had occasional locusts—but we could use the land fully. After the Dergue came to power we got the soldiers and the mines and now we can't survive even in a normal year because we can't use the land and we can't shift from the highlands to the escarpment.

In the spring of 1988 the Ethiopian army suffered major defeats and responded with a policy of civilian terror and dislocation to destroy EPLF peasant support. Thousands of self sufficient farmers in the most productive parts of Eritrea were terrorized into leaving their homes. "The Migs came early in the morning with napalm—a few lucky ones like me escaped but we lost everything." Next Page: Newly arrived refugees unload their donkey as they prepare to begin a life of uncertainty and dependence.

"At the end of 1981 the Ethiopians started to place the mines in large numbers. Whole areas of farming land were 'fenced' with mines. As the drought worsened people complained that the mines should be removed because we didn't have enough land and could not grow enough food. The Dergue said they would remove the mines if the people accepted full responsibility for any infiltration by the EPLF which meant that any EPLF infiltration would be met by the massacre of the village. It was no choice for us: the land remained mined. In our immediate area already more than fifteen people were killed accidentally by land mines but in the vicinity more than 200 people have been killed by mines. You heard explosions daily as animals stepped on the mines. Herding animals, traditionally the work of older children, became very dangerous. Sometimes a whole herd was killed because the mines were connected together and when one exploded the whole field exploded! Farming has become too dangerous."

"Everything you see in this house we got from the EPLF and ERA," Gebre Wolde and Semere, two of the first arrivals at Rora Nakfa explain in the darkness of their dugout room, "we had to leave absolutely everything behind. We always lived in fear of the Migs but when we heard troops were coming we left—that was

May 22, 1988. The She'eb massacre, where 400 people were killed—crushed with tanks and machine gunned, had taken place two weeks before. We just ran away. After a day's walk we got a ride on a truck through the EPLF. We have been two months in this place.

"We are farmers but now we are destitute—here it is not possible to farm. We were forced to leave our homes—we couldn't just wait to be killed as has happened to so many others. We are farmers but we live on food grown by others. In our home we could harvest from both the highlands and the escarpment—we could get 30-25 quintals a year—sometimes much less of course."

"I could feed my family the whole year." Semere explains. "I was a middle peasant. The escarpment was very good for cattle and we got lots of butter and sold it for cash. In a normal year it was a good life. Now it is finished."

Hollywood

Not all Eritrean refugees are destitute farmers in makeshift refugee housing; thousands of Eritreans in the diaspora are working in professional positions in the Middle East, Europe, North America—they are university professors, physicians, engineers, businessmen, phar-

Once prosperous farmers, this destitute family fled Ethiopian massacres of civilians. **Next Page:** *First steps—as a refugee. "We were farmers; we come from near the coast were land is good and we could get two crops a year. Now we are refugees. We can't grow anything here in this desert land. We break stones to build houses and wait."*

macists, publishers—virtually every profession and craft. Many have been forced to live the majority of their lives abroad and not everyone would return to Eritrea but virtually all share a commitment to Eritrean independence and they support the struggle financially.

Lia is in her early thirties, beautiful, stylish, designer glasses, coiffed. An accountant with her own firm in Hollywood, she first came to the United States as an exchange student to Beverly Hills High School. She returned briefly to Eritrea and then returned to study accounting at California State University at Northridge.

"Would I go back to Eritrea?—in a minute! You are right, an independent Eritrea could not possibly offer the material comforts I now have and after independence there will certainly be massive problems requiring self-sacrifice and a drastically lower standard of living—housing, transportation, entertainment, everything. But I am an Eritrean first—even though I have lived in America for many years I remain an Eritrean—I have never lost that. I like America: I have been successful there—but I want to return to help my people and to develop the country.

"I came to the liberated part of Eritrea to see what needed to be done and how I could contribute. Now I know—I'll return next year for three months to help upgrade accounting skills, especially computer accounting. You met the others who came with me—each of us

is a professional who contributes their time and skills to improve the infrastructure. The EPLF is far along in making the transition from a military liberation front to a government. It controls the overwhelming majority of the country and this means that everything has become larger and more complicated to administer: accounting is important for effective administration.

"This was my first time to visit the liberated areas of Eritrea—I can hardly believe what has been accomplished already—people are so self-sacrificing and patient. They ask questions until they really understand. They listen before speaking and they are thinking in the long term—what things will be like next year—in five years and more. Even though I live in exile, I can't be anything but optimistic."

"I am embarrassed for you to see me living like this, but we have lost everything."

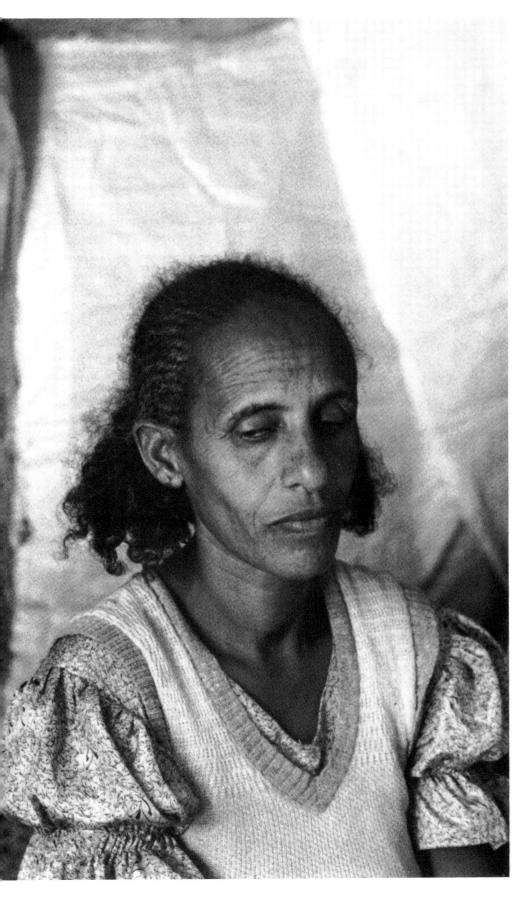

"We wait.
For years we have
waited for our
sons and daughters
to return.
We wait for
the end of the war.
We wait for
our freedom."

When they arrive most of them won't speak, don't react, withdraw from other children. It takes weeks, sometimes months for them to adjust. Their heads shaved to cure infestations, this group of orphans listens to a story from their minder.

ORPHANS

They come running
pleading:
"Are you my father?
Will you be
my father?"

Above: In a sheltered play area children learn the alphabet amid their donated playthings. *Below:* The Clinic is simple but effective.

Above: Children play on a merry-go-round made in local workshops.
Below: At the orphanage a severely withdrawn Ethiopian child is cared for. She was found alone and crying; her father was an Ethiopian officer killed by one of his own land mines as he fled an EPLF offensive.

As we eat breakfast chatting and joking at the orphanage—a collection of tents and stone-without-mortar buildings—the Eritrean radio service announces that twenty-four civilians have been murdered by Ethiopian soldiers in a village called Anseba, near the strategically important town of Keren. The Eritreans sit quietly, stone faced, as the announcer reads the names of those killed. If someone felt relief that no friends or relatives were mentioned, or a private grief on hearing familiar names it was kept inside; no one says anything. The day begins.

"Eba," the director of the orphanage whose name means "father" in Tigrinya, lies in a darkened sleeping room exhausted by fever. Friends stop to wish him well. He manages a vague malarial smile, closes his eyes and returns to semi-sleep. At thirty-one he has already been a member of the EPLF for fourteen years. The ragged scars on his chest and abdomen attest to the four years he spent as a fighter in the front lines.

Later, in a near whisper he explains: "In my village Adi Caihi, the Ethiopian army came one day and began to massacre us. They killed 85 people including my family. I joined the EPLF. After I was wounded in 1978

I started to work with orphans and have continued this work ever since."

In Eritrea there are thousands of children who have lost their mothers and fathers and who are looked after by relatives. Eba takes care of the children who have lost their entire families. They have no relatives; no one to look after them.

"After the Dergue came to power in 1974 there was a lot of massacre of civilians in the countryside especially during the Red Terror when they tried to kill all opposition. When they got the Migs the bombing killed many people and so many children lost their families. When the EPLF captured most of the towns in the middle 1970s we found a lot of children living on the streets without anyone to look after them so the EPLF started to gather the kids and take care of them, teaching them, feeding them. You can imagine what would have happened to these children if we hadn't taken them—especially the girls.

"In each military zone homeless children are taken to the Social Affairs Department. When there is a close relative of the child he is left there. When the whole family has been destroyed—and our families are quite

Left: They have everything but the candy bar. Above: Using tire casings too damaged to be retreaded youthful enthusiasm overtakes their circumstances. Next Page: Feseha, a fighter who guides visitors is mobbed by children who recognize him.

large—and there is no other alternative to look after the child they come here. We normally have about 500 children; this means 500 destroyed families. The children stay here until they are old enough to attend the boarding school where they receive up to a secondary school education.

"This camp was originally in the highlands near the town of Keren—it only had about 100 children but as the EPLF was forced to withdraw from the towns we shifted the camp to a desert area near the Sudanese border in 1979. Fortunately we were able to relocate the orphanage here in 1981. We chose this place because it had water and was relatively secure. Compared to the heat and dust of the desert it is an improvement.

"When children first arrive here they have a lot of problems; perhaps the biggest is depression. They sit alone; withdrawn, just quiet, not talking to anyone. You can see many children like this when you walk through the orphanage. This is a very difficult period for them and we have to spend a lot of time with each child. Each one is given a minder, someone who stays with the child, comforts them and talks with them and is a kind

of friend and parent but who has to explain to the child that their family is gone and won't come back and that the other children and the staff here will be their family. It is very difficult for us to do this; we don't have enough people and we are not trained to deal with these problems. We have some books and we try to understand how to treat the children but we can't replace their families; we can only offer them love and security.

"The children are divided according to their age—each group has an animal's name. For example, the youngest is the Ostrich group—these are the ones up to age three. They live together in the same tent; eat, play and attend school together. This becomes their family.

"We need clothes for the children—as you can see. We take old clothes and resew them to fit the children but we can't use all of the clothes we receive because so many children's clothes are made in bright colors; the children like them but we can't allow bright colors because they are too easily seen from the air. This is a real, not an imagined danger. In 1985, at the peak of the famine, the adjacent Solomuna refugee camp was bombed by Ethiopian Migs—throughout the day. The

Children learn early to look after themselves; pumping water using a locally made pump.

best approach for the Migs was down the narrow valley of the orphanage. Six children were killed. It took three months for the camp to return back to normal.

"When new children arrive here they all have scurvy due to lack of vitamin C and many other vitamin deficient diseases. We try very hard to provide them with proper food but we simply cannot supply enough vegetables. The Orota base area is relatively safe—at least from ground attack—but as you can see it is arid, desert mountains. We can't grow anything here and it would be too dangerous, with such a concentration of population, even if we could. You can see we have to shave the children's heads against louse infestations and all of them have sores on their legs which won't go away: mostly fungal infections. Most of them have bleeding gums. We maintain very close control over a child's health; they are weighed and examined each month—underweight kids are given special supplements of protein. We know the problems and how to cure them, but we don't have the resources."

For these children, the war will never end.

TRANSFORMATIONS

"The star is working."

*One of two wives, Amna lives a life of seclusion and
isolation. She rarely leaves the house. Her grown children
have joined the EPLF.*

WOMEN

*"It begins
at birth. . ."*

These newly arrived women refugees—shy and deferential—hear, for the first time in their lives, that they they have the right to become full members of the community. It is a long, slow process but unstoppable once begun.

"It begins at birth," explains Beseret, the Secretary of the Solomuna Refugee Settlement. "The announcement of a female birth is signalled by three 'Ulalaa'; for a male there are seven. At the birth of a boy the wife will receive many gifts from the family; for a girl she receives little. The whole family knows that the birth of a girl means a dowry will have to be paid and the girl will leave the family. A boy means wealth and continuity. As girls we had no right to go to school. This was regarded as a waste of time and a threat to our virginity. We learned to do our mother's work; fetch water, grind grain and make bread.

"Our lives were controlled by our fathers or other male relatives. We were betrothed as children to men we had never seen. Depending on our nationality we were circumcised or infibulated to keep us virgins by destroying sexual pleasure and physically closing us. At eleven or twelve we were given as brides to men of twenty or older who forced us to have sex which we didn't understand. It terrified us and often led to the wife running

away and seeking divorce which made her an outcast from her family.

"A woman had to be married to survive. We had no right to land, to engage in trading, to produce anything except crops and even this was controlled by the man. The man's family provided a house, it is true, but the wife was utterly controlled by the family. The only way to escape this was to run away to the towns but that almost always meant becoming a prostitute. That is the way it was and still is in less progressive communities."

The position of women varies within the nine nationalities which make up Eritrea: generalizations are difficult and often distortive. Women in nomadic communities tend to have the lowest status and hardest lives. Amna, herself from the lowland nomadic tradition, and now an EPLA frontline military commander, explains her transition from nomad to fighter:

"I was betrothed as a child and married at puberty to a good man. My expectations, in so far as I had any, were to subordinate myself to my husband and hope to bear male children. It is difficult for you to understand how limited our lives were—how little we knew. We

Mama Zeinab, a self taught poet of the revolution, is well known throughout Eritrea for her wit and passion.

didn't hope for a better life because there was no hope. We were fatalistic.

"My husband treated me well—according to our tradition. I bore him two children but had never looked directly into his face. It is our custom that the women never looks directly into the face of any man, even her husband. A woman must look down at the ground when talking to a man and of course I was veiled.

"I would prepare food for my husband and push it under the partition which separated the cooking area, my area, from the rest of the tent. My husband would eat and what he left me I would eat. Sometimes when he was very hungry he left me nothing.

"My life consisted of unchanging routines: then the Migs came. We were camped. I was in the tent when they came. I had never seen such a thing before—we had only heard about them. They strafed the camp and dropped fire bombs—now I know this is called napalm. I was terrified—there was so much noise and fire. I ran from the tent looking for the children and my husband. But the fire had destroyed everything including my children. When I found my husband I looked at him directly for the first time but his face was burned away by the napalm.

"In those few minutes I became destitute, alone and I had no idea what to do. When fighters from the EPLF came but I was frightened of them also. I just didn't know what to do so I went with them. That was the beginning of a new life. A life I didn't know even existed."

"Through the EPLF we have learned our enemy and our friends," explains Mama Zeinab, a Muslim woman in her sixties whose passionate poetry has become a symbol of women's emancipation and the Eritrean struggle for independence. "We have finally came out of the kitchen! We now know that our eyes, ears and tongues are normal. Before we sat veiled and silent and we knew nothing! Now we know. We are different people. It is ten times different from then! We were oppressed by the Ethiopians but we were also oppressed by our own traditions.

"A women sees everything—we saw the colonizers; we saw murder but we couldn't say anything. Now I can sit and speak with you; before my husband would have spoken with you, not me. I know about the massacre at She'eb—where the Ethiopians crushed people with tanks. Ten years ago I might know about things like this but I had to sit in silence. It is all different now. To be colonized is education; to see massacres and genocide is education. But most important was the education we got from the fighters—the EPLF. If you are taught you will

learn. I know this because even at my age I have learned. We have a saying that if you put raw meat in my stomach it will be cooked—because I am so angry. If I was young I would be a fighter and not sitting here! Tell the people in your country that it is not just Mengistu but the governments who are supporting him who cause this war. Even an old women like me knows this."

"You Can't Choose Your Own Lover"

Isa, 26, is a singer, some say the best singer, in Solomuna Camp's women's cultural troop which includes performers from each of Eritrea's nationalities.

"We lived in Asmara. My husband was an EPLF sympathizer and we feared he would be arrested so he escaped. The Dergue knew he had joined the EPLF and I was afraid they would arrest me so I escaped. This was in 1980.

"I grew up like most Eritrean women. I had an arranged marriage. In our society you can't choose your own lover. This is done by your father or uncles. But I did receive some education—up to grade three; now I am completing grade five. I am a member of the Cultural Troop of Solomuna Camp. The cultural troops are ways of expressing ourselves and bringing together the different nationalities. I play the *kerar* (Eritrean guitar) and sing. In the past women never did such things—play and sing in public. Those who did were regarded as prostitutes.

"We were all oppressed by the Ethiopian government but on the level of society my husband oppressed me. Now he is a fighter and he can accept the changes which are taking place. He encourages me to improve; he is proud of my achievements."

"I come from a village near Asmara," explains Gide, 42, "the EPLF fighters first came to the village in 1976 and began to organize the people. I went to hear the women's groups talk but my husband did not agree. He wanted me to remain in the kitchen as is our custom. But I refused because I didn't want this and I saw other women going to the meetings. This led to a lot of quarrels with my husband. In 1977 we were divorced after seven years of marriage and three children and I was pregnant with the fourth. It was a difficult time but I received a lot of support from other women and from the EPLF. In 1978 the Strategic Withdrawal took place. I was already heavily involved with the EPLF activities and I had to flee the village because the Ethiopians would surely have killed me.

"Before I was barely literate but now I am a grade four student and trained as a barefoot doctor. In 1986

Once the servants of men, women—even those whose who appear to live in the traditional way—now forcefully challenge male opinions.

The most powerful motor for social change in Eritrea is education. Once excluded from education, females now make up half of the school population.

I married a fighter. *I* chose *him*! And he understands how I have changed and what I want; he supports me. All of us, mothers and fathers, are struggling together for our rights and for the next generation. They will have the right to chose and be chosen, the right of education, the right of speaking and criticizing. That's why we are fighting for independence—not only against the Ethiopians but also against the traditions which have oppressed us."

Fatma, 32, comes from Danakil, in the eastern lowlands. Her friends at Solomuna come from nationalities she didn't know existed.

"I am a Tigre by nationality. I grew up in the traditional way and was betrothed at fifteen. In the 1960s my husband joined the ELF and we were caught up in the fighting between ELF and EPLF. In 1970 we got married but within a few days my husband had to flee and I didn't see him again for six years—then we met for a few days in the liberated areas.

"I also had to run away because the Ethiopians knew my husband had joined the ELF and it became too dangerous for me to stay. I came to Solomuna

Young women growing up in Eritrea today learn early to associate with men as friends and colleagues.

Camp. When I arrived here I had never been to school. Now I am in grade 3. In my nationality I am a part of a man's property. Now I am free of that and I have the right to speak and participate in community affairs. If you are not educated you know nothing and nothing is expected of you. If you are educated you have the responsibility to educate others. In traditional society I would rarely even be seen—it was my position to avoid being seen by others. Like my friends I am training to be a barefoot doctor."

Fatna is 38 years old and lives with her husband and children in the village of Bikla at Rora Habab in the Eritrean highlands, a community which is rapidly transforming itself. Her traditional appearance belies a strong minded woman who is able to reconcile traditional and modern social roles:

"So many women lost their husbands because of the war and the political persecutions. These women couldn't just go to Sudan to work like men do. They had a very hard time. When the community created the Village Assembly with the help of the EPLF and decided to start the self-help projects with support from ERA,

women got equality of opportunity to participate with the men. This had never happened before: our lives really began to change.

"In the past we spent half of each day carrying water—just doing that! This was especially difficult for women without husbands or whose husbands had gone to Sudan to work and who had many other things to do, especially if they had small children. Imagine spending half of your time carrying water!

"Each day we also had to grind the grain into flour. This is hard work and very time consuming.

"Now we have the dams and the wells. This means I can carry enough water for my family in fifteen minutes instead of 3-4 hours! And we have the mill. My grain can be ground into flour in a few minutes rather than hours. For the first time women have the *time* to participate in the affairs of the community. We have time to get education and we are encouraged to go to school. I am now beginning grade two. I can read and write and tell time. I am learning mathematics this year.

"School is important and many adult women are attending—far more women than men—but we also

Left: Women are now being educated in every type of profession and trade in Eritrea. The first graduating class of the Wina Technical School was 55 percent women. **Below:** A driver, Mebrat is responsible for carefully maintaining "her" Land Cruiser. **Next Page:** The electronics repair shop is responsible for maintaining a wide variety of equipment from simple radios to computers.

have time to take better care of our fields. We are terracing them, planting trees, weeding them better and growing new vegetables which we never had before. Life is really changing for all of us, especially for women. There is so much more to know than carrying water and grinding flour."

No visitor to Eritrea can help but be impressed by the contrast between the position of women in traditional societies and in the EPLF or the communities in the process of transformation. An oft-quoted Eritrean proverb illustrates the traditional view of women: "Just as there is no donkey with horns, so there is no woman with brains." How did this change?

Professor Bereket: "One has to remember the EPLF was formed at a time when there was a movement for women to gain equality in much of the world and this attitude was shared by Eritrean students and teachers. But our commitment to improving women's position wasn't entirely inspired by the feminist movement in the United States although that obviously was one of the factors. There was, of course, the larger national historical context of Eritrean women traditionally holding a subordinate position to men which we have all seen in our personal lives. We have mothers and sisters and some of us, wives; we knew the position of women. It was not difficult for some of us to realize the importance of liberating women from these age old restraints, not

only in terms of justice demanding it, but in terms of the efficacy of the movement; women are one half of the population. If one half of your population is continually denied equality it will undermine your movement. It is as simple as that."

Secretary General Isaias adds, "The political atmosphere of the 1960s played some role but we also drew on our own traditions. We have a diversity of societies with often contradictory traditions and cultures. The Kunamas are a *very* traditional society but women have strong roles in certain areas. Among the Afars, in the south, this is also the case. This is a part of the Eritrean tradition even though it is limited to certain areas and societies which we have built on and which has not been inspired by ideas from outside.

"This is also true when it comes to the land holding and land tenure systems in Eritrea. In the majority of societies women are prohibited from owning land but in certain areas of the highlands women are permitted to hold land. It is important for us to be able to point to these practices when it comes to formulating policies within the EPLF—and to expand these traditional practices, which we regard as positive for women, in the programs we develop.

"Why is the participation of women in modernization so prominent in Eritrea?

Traditionally women were banned from money-earning crafts such as weaving. At Solomuna Camp they are encouraged to become economically self-sufficient by weaving the gabi, the soft cotton shawl worn by men and women. **Next Page:** Wrapped in a shroud-like cloth, a fighter sleeps through the day; at nightfall, when it is safe to travel, she will deliver emergency medical supplies.

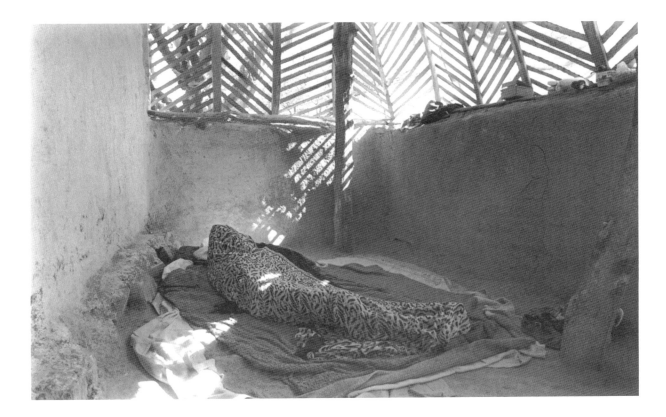

"There are many schools of thought; maybe women are more ready to change than men. You would never think a woman could be equal to a man in our traditional way of thinking. But our experience has taught us that women, although perhaps physically weaker—when it comes to being courageous or bearing up, women are equal to men—in some cases, they are superior. Often they are *more* responsible than men.

"Women have eagerly taken up educational programs—more than men. Women want to go to school, they want to get out of their kitchens. When we began to talk to communities we said: 'Look it is not the EPLF which forbids you from going to school: it is your men and your traditions.' Women had to decide what they wanted to do about that. Often there would be an 'uprising' of women in a village; they would demand to go to school. From this beginning women soon demanded to participate in village assemblies and in civic life. The EPLF did not create these desires; we only offered women the chance to fulfill them. If the women themselves had not wanted this, nothing would have happened.

"Another element in the change of women's roles has been the intensification of the political struggle. We are a small nation of 3.5 million people. The struggle for survival, the struggle to implement our programs—if we had relied on only one section of our society, leaving

aside women, it would not have been achieved. In every aspect of our struggle we try to involve as many of our people as possible and that includes women."

Bereket: "As the EPLF became larger in 1975-76 when thousands of young women joined with their men compatriots as fighters and in the professional services, the importance of women's equality in the movement was emphasized. Even the traditionalist die-hards had to admit that women can perform functions equal to men. From then on in was not so difficult to accept women's equality in principle. However, one has to draw a distinction between the EPLF and the broader society. Among the nomadic populations in northern and western Eritrea and even in the agricultural societies, women remained subordinated. A movement of this kind created a challenge to society at large and disrupted the expectations of the older generation who watched with interest as women, carrying Kalashnikov assault rifles, defeated Ethiopian soldiers. This helped create a sense of heroism about womanhood. Social changes were taking place not because we had leaders dictating "this is the way" but it was experience and the performance of women themselves which ultimately changed peoples' minds.

"The fact of the Ethiopian occupation of our towns meant that many of our women were actually forced into marriages and some of them were raped by Ethiopian officers and soldiers and that of course was a traumat-

At the Solomuna Camp, adult women who once arrived as destitute refugees and who have already completed primary education learn anatomy, part of their course to become barefoot doctors.

Women trainee welders peer out of their tool shed made from recycled, captured Ethiopian ammunition cases—a major source of construction wood.

ic experience which drove some of them to joining their brothers in the EPLF. The end result of that has strengthened and enriched the Eritrean struggle and made it unique in this respect. One-third of the EPLF is women.

"When people were able to live safely behind the EPLF lines—families began to settle in villages like Solomuna. The fighters protected the villages and the villages protected and nurtured the fighters. A guerrilla force was transformed into a whole society fighting together. This would not have been possible without developing a policy of respect and equality towards women."

National Union of Eritrean Women

Worku is in her early thirties and is a member of the executive committee of the Research and Information Department of the National Union of Eritrean Women. The Union, with 50,000 members, has branches in Eritrea, the Middle East, Europe and North America and promotes policies of specific concern to women. She identifies the problems which the National Union of Eritrean Women seeks to overcome:

"At birth females are not welcomed either by the family or the society. They are regarded as men's property. A woman has no right to go to school. She is socialized in a completely different way from men. She is taught to be passive, obedient and subsurvient.

"A woman is forced to marry before the age of puberty. Her marriage is arranged by the father or male relatives. Men also have arranged marriages but they can reject the woman if they wish. A woman is supposed to be a virgin at marriage. In order to ensure this women are circumcised and/or infibulated.

"In married life the husband has the right to make all decisions. A man can divorce. In the highlands a woman can divorce but this is decided by the family and if they say no she must remain. A man can divorce for no reason in the lowlands. He takes the children with him if wishes. In divorce a woman has no property rights. She cannot own property and she cannot inherit.

"Traditionally a woman is not allowed to attend the meetings of the community. In many societies she is not allowed to go out of the house or associate with people—even in the church, which is segregated.

"The changes began with the EPLF which wanted to modernize Eritrean society and it was not possible to do this while ignoring 50 percent of the population. In this way women became involved in the struggle. The EPLF assigned members to work among the women using different means with different societies. In some societies they were not allowed to attend the meetings and seminars and we had to talk individually with women to discuss the causes of their problems and how to deal with them.

"In 1973 the first women joined the armed struggle. In 1976-77 the first Womens Associations were formed at the village, district and regional level. In June 1979 the National Union of Eritrean Women was formed. This was just one of the organizations which the

*In the frigid highlands at Rora Habab—a community which is in the process of transforming itself—traditional and modern roles of women (**Next Page**) coexist as a woman prepares coffee while learning to tell time, part of her primary education.*

EPLF founded to give particular sections of Eritrean society a forum to discuss their problems and ideas and to bring them into the policy formation process. The Union shouldered the task of mobilizing and organizing women.

"We have six areas where we seek to improve the position of women: socially by improved education and combating gender discrimination, legally through land and marriage law, in employment and wages, improved health care—especially for mother and child, to organize women to be an effective political force—at present there are six women on the Central Committee of the EPLF (out of seventy-one members)—and to connect our movement with other progressive women's movements internationally.

"Eighty-five percent of Eritrean women are still illiterate—a reduction of ten percent since the mid 1970s; obviously not good enough, but a start. In 1983 we started a large scale literacy program. Twenty seven thousand women started but the intensification of the war and then the famine meant that only 9,000 completed the first phase. It is difficult to talk about education, development, consciousness-raising when people are starving—1984-85 was a terrible period.

"The basic idea of the EPLF to change society met a great deal of resistance both from men and women,

especially the older generations: Muslims in particular felt some of the changes violated Muslim law, the *sharia.* EPLF representatives were even arrested by local communities. Women would not show up as promised for meetings. We had to gather religious leaders to discuss the *sharia* and show that the *sharia* does not prohibit the education of women nor does it require the circumcision and infibulation of women as many Muslims honestly believe. Some people are still not convinced. But we are not prepared to allow women to be victimized any longer because of ignorance. We try to persuade communities that women now have basic rights and if, for example, a woman is denied the right to education, we, the EPLF, enforce her rights. How? We first try to persuade those opposed that this is the right thing to do: that society is changing and that women are a part of these changes. If they refuse we will punish them by making them work on farms or other projects.

"We also have a number of specific projects underway. We promote small economic enterprises—we are starting a small jam workshop at Nacfa trying to use the plentiful wild cactus fruit. We have handicraft workshops to help women develop artisanal skills like weaving and machine-sewing from which they have been traditionally excluded. The EPLF helps us to fund these projects as do outside non-governmental donor groups. We are also

Rora Habab's farmers still face decades of agricultural insecurity due to irregular rains and decades of severely degraded soils. The community has planned and is carrying out a self-help project of land terracing (funded by aid organizations and ERA), the first step to ecological rehabilitation.

working with displaced women—many of the displaced people are women with small children. Often their husbands have been killed and they are desperate and without support. And we are conducting research about women. If we are to have effective planning and policies we need to have detailed information about the situation of women in each area of Eritrea.

"We are only at the beginning of what will be a long process of consciousness-raising and social change but we have made some gains: women are 52 percent of the laboratory technicians, 20 percent of the X-ray technicians, 50 percent of medical photographers, 20 percent of the barefoot doctors, 15 percent of the doctors, 22 percent of the machine workers, 49 percent of the leather workers, to name just a few areas where women are now participating. You have to remember the women started from zero!

"Women have now achieved a new legal status within the EPLF—we hope that one day all civilian communities will adopt it and we intend it to be the basis of women's rights in an independent Eritrea. Women cannot be discriminated against because of their

gender, they are able to own and inherit land and other property which is particularly important in the case of divorce where, in the past, women had no rights and were left destitute. The 1978 marriage law prohibits child marriages and requires that *both* parties to an adult marriage give their consent. We are working with civilian communities to abolish female circumcision and infibulation, which are major health hazards for women, and some communities, admittedly few, have already stopped these practices.

"If our development projects are going to be meaningful the war has to come to an end. The war has drastically affected women—many men are away or have been killed and women are both mothers and the head of the family now. Mothers have watched their children die in the famine; they have starved, been raped, lost their shelter, clothing, food. The National Union of Eritrean Women demands that the international community find a political solution to the war. Ethiopia doesn't want this but the world could pressurize them—instead it turns a deaf ear."

Due to insufficient water Rora's farmers have been forced to leave their farms and families for part of the year and seek work in Sudan for pitiful wages. With this new dam built by the EPLF Construction Department, crops can be irrigated throughout the year and migration is no longer necessary.

The success of Rora Habab stems from its grassroots community participation and tangible improvements in individual lives. Members of the community who participate in the project gather to evaluate the progress of the reforestation plan. Each participant is accountable to the group for his or her performance.

Transfixed by her own image, seen perhaps for the first time, this refugee girl who has survived the destruction of her village can hardly know the new possibilities which await her.

In their thorn tree "school," using books prepared by the Education Department and printed by the Information Department, children struggle to learn to read their native language, Tigrinya.

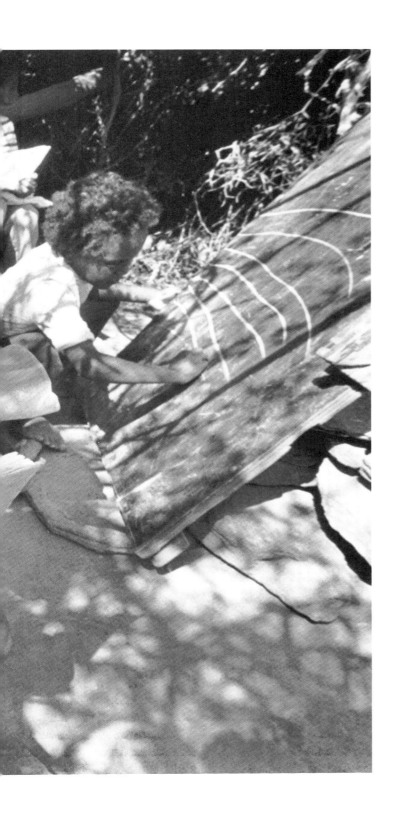

EDUCATION

*"When you are educated,
you have the
responsibility
to educate others."*

Above: School bells of artillery and machine gun casings. Below: Amidst massive boulders, which offer camouflage and protection from air attack, children attend school.

It is 3:00 A.M. on a moonless night and we have been driving since dusk. A light flickers and we stop, a few words are exchanged and a young fighter climbs into the Land Cruiser carrying a copy of O'Neil's *Bolshevik Experience.* A hour later we stop and he departs into the darkness without a word. Everyone in Eritrea seems to possess two things: an AK-47 and a book.

Andeberhan, is the Harvard-educated deputy director of the Education Department: "As you know we are at war; a war of national liberation. But we are engaged in another war; the war to transform the traditional society of Eritrea. In this process education plays an important role. When you talk about changing society, we are first and foremost talking about changing people; particularly people's ideas of themselves, of their society and their environment. In this respect, education for us is an instrument of liberation; no less than the gun. Through education we try to eradicate illiteracy; we try to bring about the cultural development of our people. We try to replace traditional, suspicious ideas that are inherent in a backward society like ours and replace them with a scientific understanding of the world.

"Education is also a part of our strategy of integrated development. Although our education programs have both theoretical and practical components, ultimately they must meet our requirements for national reconstruction.

"At the moment we have 165 schools and 1,782 teachers with about 27,000 students inside Eritrea. We offer education to fighters and civilians in the liberated areas and clandestinely behind the lines. We offer primary through secondary school academic education as well as technical education. In cooperation with other depart-

Right: Teachers' "room" at Janni school. *Below:* A "classroom" equipped with locally produced tables, chairs and schoolroom furniture. "We don't want to teach like this; we are fighting to have proper schools where children can learn in safety."

ments we prepare and print all of the nearly eighty different textbooks used in the schools.

"The Education Department has sections responsible for different aspects of our programs. For example, we have a research and development section which is responsible for reviewing the educational program and materials every five years in the light of feedback we get from students, teachers and the community through the Village Assemblies. We have very limited resources and we operate under difficult conditions of war and drought—it is essential to make our educational system efficient and relevant to our situation."

Through the Eritrean Relief Association (ERA) education is being transformed into development. ERA is in the frontline of the transformations taking place in Eritrea.

"We plan projects in response to local initiatives," says ERA's soft spoken Lilo, an agricultural economist trained at the University of Wisconsin. "We do not go to areas and announce projects. Local communities, with help from the various departments of the EPLF, organize themselves as self-governing units, define priorities, and then ask the civilian departments of the EPLF to help in developing projects to meet their needs. Surveys are done with the research and development unit of each concerned department—health, education, etc. The proposed project is submitted to the Economic Planning Commission which coordinates all projects and sets

Hundreds of children like these—orphans, children of fighters and others attend classes through secondary level. Among the subjects they study are Eritrean and world history, sciences, and foreign languages, principally English and Arabic.

priorities. Once a project is approved it is allocated resources—when we have them—and goes forward. Rora Habab is such a project."

Rora Habab

Located at 2500 meters in the Eritrean highlands, about 640 families are voluntarily taking part in the project, out of a total population of about 15,000. The objective is to make them as self-reliant as possible but the project was only begun in 1986 and progress, while dramatic, is still localized.

"The most important immediate problem at Rora Habab is to try to reverse decades of ecological deterioration which will improve productive capacities and allow people to stay at Rora throughout the year. We are not attempting to totally change their lifestyle. At present, in the summer the people live in Rora but in the winter they emigrate to the coastal areas. They do not migrate because they want to do this; ecological-economic circumstances force them to migrate. The key to successful planning at Rora is the participation of the people in *all*

Yosief, an Addis Ababa-trained lawyer, already a decade with the EPLF, listens to an EPLF news radio broadcast. Even in remote areas, Eritreans are well informed about world affairs via the EPLF radio and BBC World Service. On the wall behind him are covers of some of the eighty different school books printed by the Information Department.

aspects of the planning—designing, constructing and implemention of projects.

"Rora is a plateau and has severe water shortage problems especially during winter. We have had to learn how to harvest water, not mine it. Wells are not effective in this area: we have to catch the water in dams. The Construction Department built a large earth dam which now provides drinking water for people and water for animals. The dam allows people to keep livestock in this area the entire year and that could mean further ecological deterioration through overgrazing. We must be watchful. On the other hand the secure supply of water means that a part of the family can remain behind even when the animals are taken out during the winter, which allows a continuity of education and health services which otherwise would be impossible.

"The community is working hard on terracing and reforestation to improve the basic ecology of the area after years of neglect and destructive agricultural-grazing practices. We have to think in terms of 10-20 years of work—there are no easy or short-term answers to these problems.

"So far the project has made changes which we have not yet had an opportunity to evaluate sufficiently—the social impact. The community has built three schools and is planning another. The schools are used by

In cramped underground workshop textbooks are assembled by hand. Next page: The Information Department makes extensive use of video to show Eritreans living abroad how their financial contributions make the revolution possible.

children and adults. Most of the adult students are women on whom education is having an important liberating and emancipating impact.

"While the civilian departments of the EPLF and the ERA provide advice and material contributions the project is self-generated, self-governed and all labor costs are the responsibility of the community. There is a monthly meeting of participants which assesses the previous month's work and sets the program for the following month. Work groups of 7-10 take the responsibility to carry out parts of the work load. For example one group has the responsibility to carry out measures against army worm, an insect which destroys crops. Other groups are busy with reforestation—encouraging people to plant trees and to tend them, protecting them from animals and pests. Others are concerned with the building of pit latrines—an absolutely essential part of the water catchment system. Without latrines it is not possible to collect clean run-off water in the dams and catchment basins. Yet others are concerned with the introduction of new crops, especially vegetables and potatoes.

"The project combines a number of EPLF civilian departments although in this case the Agriculture Department is the overall project coordinator linking together Public Health, Education, Public Administration, Agriculture (seed, oxen distribution), Social Affairs, Construction, Transportation and Education. All policy decisions and the responsibility for carrying out project goals lie with the community."

"Before the project we had to move to get grass for the animals," Tzaid explains. "Between December and May we went to Sahel in search of grazing. In May we returned here and farmed. But some went as far as Sudan working as day laborers on the big commercial farms near Tokar or in Port Sudan, leaving their families behind and only returning during the planting season. But the work is erratic in Port Sudan and depends on how many ships need to be off- or on-loaded. You might work two or three days and then wait a week. In three months, if you were lucky, you could earn 330 Sudanese pounds [US$27.00], enough to buy some clothes and coffee. In a good year you would earn enough to buy a sack of wheat. One advantage of going to Tokar is that you could take the family along and maybe the women and children could get some work.

"We only do this out of economic necessity. The agricultural yields were becoming smaller and smaller and the animals were giving less and less milk. During the drought years it was very bad. Until 1981 it wasn't so bad but after that it got worse. In 1982-84 it was a disaster. The drought was very strong following years of drought, and we received very little food help then. We started to receive food aid at the end of 1984 and things got a little better. People who owned ten cattle before the drought lost everything or perhaps managed to save one cow.

"Being in the project is much better. We received seeds and tools. Before we moved from place to place in search of food. Food aid means we can settle in one area and build up our farms. The hardships of going here and there—which we did because we had no choice—are relieved.

"We have solved the problem of water. We *all* participated in the water project—even those who did

The Photography Section is systematically documenting the changes taking place in Eritrea in addition to providing basic photographic services. Photographers struggle with the layout problems of a book they are preparing.

not want to participate in other parts of the project—everyone benefits, even the nomads.

"Because more and more people are able to remain here the whole year we have been able to improve other services. We have health care, especially better trained midwives and veterinary care. We now have dams and wells and better agricultural practices like terracing and new crops like vegetables which were never grown before. We have a blacksmith and a tailor and a mill for grinding grain. We have learned about all of these things from education and we want our children to get a modern education in Tigre, our language, but also to study Arabic and English. They need to learn mathematics and science and hygiene. We didn't get this before."

Lilo goes on to explain that it has not all been success; huge problems remain and the question of how to accommodate nomads into modern Eritrea still has no answer.

"When the war is over we will make a land use survey to establish priorities. Nomads and pastoralists have a place in Eritrea. We do not want to settle all nomads. A lot of our land is barren but suitable for migratory pastoralists. We hope over the long term to encourage mixed farming but many areas don't allow mixed farming and resettlement is only possible on the basis of free choice.

"The Agraa irrigated agricultural project started on an emergency basis in 1985. Its goal was to grow large amounts of food rapidly to save lives threatened by the famine; secondarily we wanted to introduce nomads, who are the most vulnerable to famine, to farming. After two years we evaluated the project. It is not very successful because it is too expensive and too complicated and local people cannot maintain it, but it did save many lives. We asked the people who had settled at Agraa if they would like to stay or return to nomadism. Seventy percent wanted to return to their old way of life—most therefore will leave when climatic conditions permit it.

"Agraa taught us other things—about the problems of generalizing pilot projects. Agraa was and is unique but we are too poor to create such capital intensive, complex projects. Of course ERA could operate the project. We could guarantee success if we run it, if success is measured solely in increased crop production, but we don't want this kind of dependency—success for us means self-reliance and it is not realistic to think that projects like Agraa can be self-reliant under these conditions. We need to develop projects which can realistically be operated by local people."

A new generation of Eritrean women is emerging. Not all are joining the EPLF but all are benefiting from its reforms.

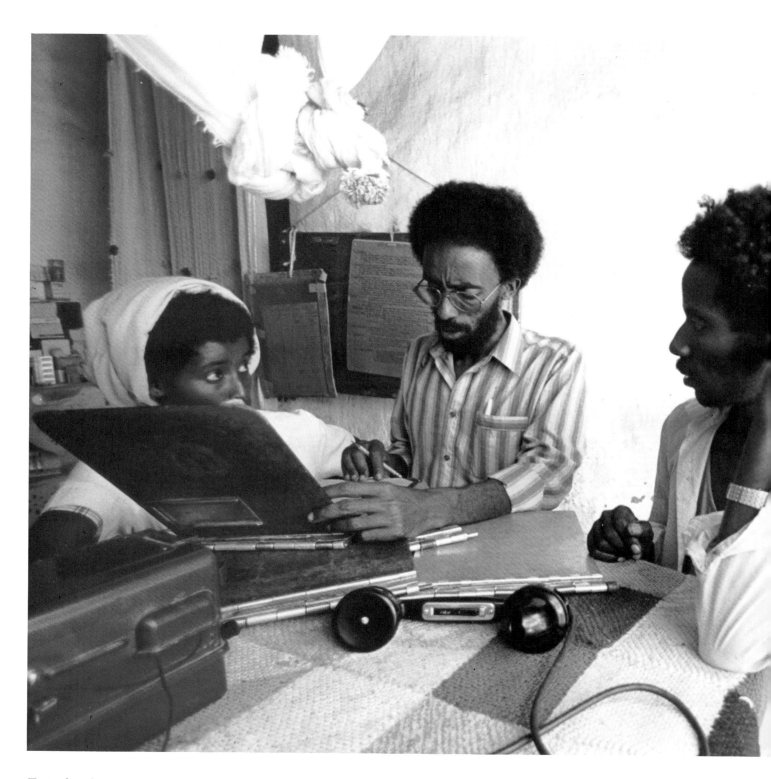

Trained at the University of Addis Ababa, cardiovascular
surgeon Dr. Michaeli Gebrehiwot works seven-day weeks
with too many patients and insufficient supplies.

HEALTH

*"Health is not the
absence of disease;
it is the enjoyment of well-being,
whatever it means—
this is a philosophical
and moral question."*

It is late afternoon. Dr. Michaeli, the head of cardiovascular surgery in the main hospital in the Orota base area, walks into the operating room, places a cassette into the radio cassette player on the concrete floor and punches the "play" button. As the first bars of the aria of Glenn Gould's eclectic performance of Bach's Goldberg Variations drifts from the speakers, he begins what will be a night of surgery lasting until the early morning. "In the field" with the EPLF for 14 years, Dr. Michaeli is married to a nurse. They live in a camouflaged one-room house made of unmortared stone.

"A typical day begins at 7:00 when I make rounds of the wards. This usually lasts about two hours and then I change bandages and inspect the wounds. After that I have the polyclinic which other colleagues attend as well as our trainees—I think you know we are training our own personnel from primary health care workers through beginning surgeons. This usually lasts until lunch. All food, for patients and staff, is prepared in the Central Hospital Kitchen to save firewood, which is a very serious problem for us. Since the variety of foods available to us are very limited we all eat the same meals.

"In the afternoon I have a teaching routine; some days it is surgical nurses, other days the barefoot doctors. Nurses who have already had a decade of operating room experience are trained to perform simple operations and they can do much repair and many stabilization procedures.

"I begin surgery after dusk, when it is safe to turn on the generators. We work until we are finished. We have developed many of our own anaesthetic and surgical procedures adapted to our limited resources and situation. The necessity to camouflage, to restrict certain care to the night hours, to disperse the hospital some four miles along the valley imposes inefficiencies which we cannot overcome until we have peace.

"Outside support groups and the Eritrean exile refugee community have helped us to offer reasonable health care here in the hospital. For example the Belgian support group raised money to help build the laboratory which makes sterile intravenous infusions—the one you saw housed in the two converted shipping containers. We are quite proud of our manufacturing pharmacy."

"On infusions, we save over 50 percent—compared to buying them," explains Senai, the chief pharmacist, "on tablets up to 40 percent; on capsules we save just over 25 percent. Overall we save about 45 percent of our pharmaceutical costs by manufacturing here inside Eritrea rather than importing finished drugs. On some drugs the savings runs to 70 percent. The war consumes

Left: "Our hospital isn't the best in the world but it is the longest." It runs along the valley floor for about four miles, dug into hillsides, camouflaged under acacia trees, sometimes built into shipping containers when absolute sterility is necessary. *Above:* Evaluating x-rays and cardio-encephalograms in his "polyclinic" made of old tents, is only one small part of a punishing work day. At dusk, once the danger of air attack has passed and the generators can be started, Dr. Michaeli starts surgery: if he is lucky he will finish by 2:00 A.M. in time to sleep a few hours before his day starts again with rounds at 7:00 A.M.

Right: Dr. Michaeli's camouflaged home, which he shares with his wife, a nurse, is one room built dug into the side of the valley. *Below:* Making "rounds" with his students Dr. Michaeli questions them about the appropriate diagnosis and treatment. "We have no choice: we have to train our own medical staff."

about 55 percent of what we produce. If we could redirect this to the civilian population it would make a significant difference."

"The pharmacy was started in 1984," Senai continues, "and has gone from producing nothing to our current level of production which, as the new capsule machine comes on line for the antibiotics, will total several million tablets per year. We have quite ambitious plans based on the success of the current pharmacy which includes expanding production to new drugs, hopefully a plastic container workshop to solve some of our packaging problems. We work in a very hostile environment and proper packaging is essential to prevent waste. We intend to produce injectable solutions and the oral rehydration unit is already planned. Everything needs to be bigger, faster, and produce more."

Plastic Microscopes

Earlier in London I had asked about the piles of bulging plastic garbage bags in the cramped EPLF office.

Above: The central kitchen of the Orota hospital. "We are lucky to have anything at all: patients and staff eat the same food." *Below:* As we prepare to eat lunch Dr. Michaeli just smiles when I ask him about special diets.

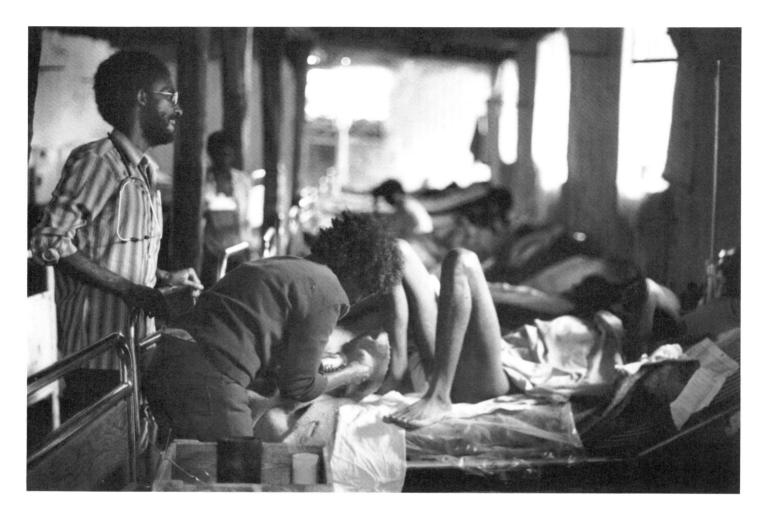

In one of his wards (thinly plastered mud brick walls, earth floor, corrugated tin roof and yet remarkably clean) Dr. Michaeli jokes with recovering fighters.

"Oh those are microscopes" Petros explained in passing.

Microscopes in plastic trash bags?

"We needed an inexpensive microscope for the Health Service. A normal microscope costs about $500. The Eritrean microscope costs $70. At this price no company wanted to produce it. It was expensive to make the moulds and so 10,000 units were produced—the bags are full of parts. About 200 have been fully assembled and sent to Eritrea. Obviously other countries need such a microscope and we intended to produce them for our needs and sell them in the Third World. Ironically we have had only limited success because the World Health Organization and other international organizations won't endorse it, due to Ethiopian pressure, because it says Eritrean Health Service on it and we are regarded as a secessionist movement."

Dr. Nerayo, head of pediatrics and one of the founders of the Eritrean Health Service (EHS), has been a leader in health care planning in Eritrea for more than a decade.

Considering the conditions under which it has to function, The Eritrean Health Service is uncommonly efficient. One reason is the hospital's Blood Transfusion Service and the Central Pharmacy which produces top quality tablets and capsules.

"In 1984 the Eritrean Health Service produced a document outlining primary health care in the rural areas. We thought that in five or six years there would be primary health care coverage to 80-90 percent of the population. However, the intensification of the war and famine have dictated against this. But essentially things are moving towards this goal—by 1994-95 we should have a fully functioning health service serving about 80-90 percent of the total population. At the moment, we are serving something like a quarter of the population and we are giving some kind of service to something like two-thirds of the population.

"The basic principle of the Eritrean Health Service is that health services goes to the people rather than the people coming to the health service. Everything is organized on this preventive health care principle; no third world country can afford to operate an acute care system—I would question whether many developed countries can afford this as well."

As he explains the structure of the EHS, Dr. Assafaw, a 1972 gradute from Haile Selassie University's medical school and current head of the civilian hospital

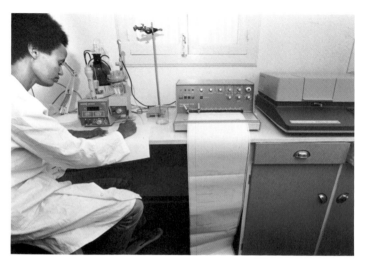

"Our equipment ranges from a quite sophisticated high speed capsule making machine to an sterile intravenous solutions production unit (above) housed in a 'building' made of two shipping containers, but we also make simple disinfectants and fill the bottles by hand. We are able to meet our basic drug needs at a fraction of cost of imported finished drugs."

in Orota, cages cigarettes from visitors since he receives no salary and can't buy them. Theoretically he works a six-day week; actually he works whenever necessary.

"The medical service was started from scratch but at the moment we have 385 village level clinics with two health workers in each serving about 500 people. We also have forty mobile teams made up of medical assistants and advanced barefoot doctors. The mobile teams service nomadic communities which are not settled in villages. For each ten villages we have a health station. At the next level we have twenty-two regional health centers and then we have ten regional hospitals where surgical, gynecological, obstetric and other services are available. At the top we have the Central Hospital where you are now. This has recently been divided into military and civilian sections. At the civilian hospital we currently have about 300 patients but many more come during periods of combat. In the surgical section at least half of our patients are war wounded.

"We have made great strides in the past years and we have built up quite a momentum, but we have really only begun. We estimate that 2,500 village health workers are necessary and we have trained about 10 percent of these. We need 3,500 traditional birth attendants and we are training them as circumstances and supplies allow."

Dr. Nerayo continues: "The most important health workers in Eritrea are community health workers who have a very basic health knowledge but are doing most of the work because 75-80 percent of our health problems are common diseases which can be prevented with limited resources and knowledge. At the sub-district level we have a clinic where four or five people are working and there we offer a minimum laboratory service—not more than 8-10 tests, for parasites, etc.—but this is a tremendous achievement.

Health Care Must Be Appropriate

"Health is not the absence of disease it is the enjoyment of well being whatever it means—this is a philosophical and moral question as well as a strictly medical question. We have problems of nutrition, hygiene, pure water, common infections, parasitical infections, problems of the mother and child, childbirth. This is a list of diseases

and problems which are first, easily preventable, and second, easily curable with primary health care. Of course, hidden in this argument is that the primary health care be appropriate. We must resist expensive hospitalization which, in most third world countries, serves only a very small, privileged sector of the population. The majority of the population who are responsible for the economic development of the country are forgotten. The health care system must be appropriate. It should be inexpensive—at present it is entirely free. It should easily available to everyone.

"We have to be very realistic. We are living in a society distorted by war. When peace comes there will be a change of values. But I am optimistic that whatever changes come later on, there is so much community involvement in the health services and the community has seen for itself the positive results, that they will continue to support it after independence. There will always be some problems. I am sure there will be doctors coming from outside with the latest equipment, someone who will want to set up a private clinic, but I think this will be the exception which we will have to accommo-date. These will almost certainly be true in the cities: in the EHS we stress programs which serve the needs of the rural population."

"Look at the health care problems we face," Dr. Assafaw continues, "The average age in Eritrea is thirty-eight. Four hundred and twenty-five children out of 1,000 die before one year. Since the Soviet intervention in the war in 1978 the number of casualties has increased twenty times. In 1986-87 we treated over 3,000 war injured civilians. Napalm is used widely against civilians and leads to horrendous injuries which take a great deal of time to heal and are very expensive to treat. We have more than 600,000 displaced people inside Eritrea. In the three months after the fall of Afabet [March 1988] we had between 50,000-90,000 newly displaced people. Most disease is linked to the conditions of life: war, displacement, malnutrition, infections, TB, gastroenteritis, anemia, malaria. In the lowlands, among the nomadic populations women are particularly malnourished in times of shortage; men take as much food as they want to keep up their strength and women get what is left over—if there is anything. We

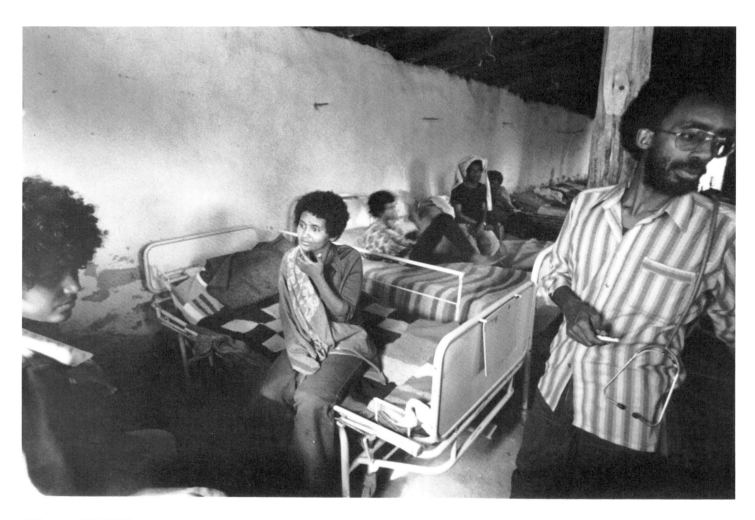

face annual epidemics—in the lowlands this year we had over 1,000 cases of meningitis between January-April. Untreated meningitis has a mortality rate of 96 percent. We need to inoculate 200,000 people but we were only able to inoculate 30,000 because of a lack of supplies and the difficulties of keeping the cold chain intact between Europe and Eritrea to protect the vaccine.

"We are not just fighting medical problems. We are also fighting backwardness, poverty, drought, insect infestations, and of course war. We have made achievements in the struggle but its not enough. Yes, we have now thirty-five full certified doctors in a variety of specialities, thirty-seven semi-trained (locally) surgeons, one hundred fifty nurses, sixty lab technicians and sixty fully trained midwives. Our ability to work immediately behind the front during combat has meant that our mortality rate is less than 15 percent which is quite good considering the difficult conditions and limited supplies."

Nerayo continues: "Our health care problems derive from a complicated interaction of factors: social, economic, military, political but fully trained physicians and expensive hospitals cannot solve these problems. You

Previous Page: Too many patients, not enough time, not enough supplies. **Above:** *One of Dr. Michaeli's responsibilities is to train barefoot doctors. "Most civilian health problems we face can be handled by this level of health care worker. Our success in training our own people to deal with war wounds is a major element in our very low rate of fighter mortality."*

Agnash is a locally trained midwife whose simple, spotlessly clean delivery room offers women a safe alternative to traditional birthing methods in which a quarter of the women die.

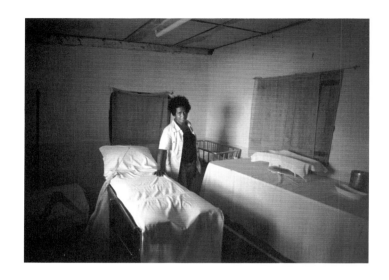

will meet diseases which require a fully trained physicians but most of our health care problems can be treated by lesser trained people. For example, most cases of malaria can be treated by a person who is illiterate. There are some cases of malaria which require a fully qualified physician because there are complications—cerebral malaria for example.

"Most ailments have important psychological elements. If you have two patients having the same number of bacterial infections one can be very sick and the other can be relatively well; it depends how he feels. What is his perception of disease? This is a very important, that the patient gives you an adequate idea of his perception of the disease. It does not follow that more drugs are the answer. A doctor must gain the confidence of his patient and try to make him feel better by changing the image of the disease."

Dr. Assafaw: "Do we need doctors? We have over thirty now and 70-80 would be enough for what we could realistically do at present. What we really need are trained primary health care workers. The vast majority of medical problems could be addressed by this level of health care worker."

Dr. Michaeli: "Delivering health care is a very slow process—especially among the nomads. At first they allowed only the children to be treated—after all they are the most expendable and often died anyway. Adults were too important. When health workers first contacted nomads they also preached against female circumcision, infibulation and clitorectomy—they were driven away. We still talk about these things but now only after

communities have accepted others elements of the EPLF health care program.

"Often it is the women who pushed for the new health care—so many die in childbirth. Now they come to the hospitals or clinics to deliver. At first the traditional values of nomadic society made health care difficult. Women could not speak for themselves; we could not touch a woman. Their men described their symptoms.

"As the first successes were apparent, especially in childbirth, but also more generally, the nomads began to come to the hospital, often asking for a specific test they had heard about from others or an x-ray. The x-ray became a symbol of effective treatment and many wanted it. We often gave it to them in order to build up their confidence and respect in us. This worked and more and more people came to the clinics and hospitals. Eventually women began to speak for themselves and men brought their families for care; leaving them here at the hospital while they returned to tend their animals. The nomads learned that their families would be safe here at the hospital.

"Once we had established this basic trust we could talk more widely about our policies which conflicted with traditional nomad views. We discovered that younger women were generally opposed to infibulation, clitorectomy and polygamy, practices which the EPLF wishes to abolish. We know we can't force people to stop this—there is no way to enforce it—it has to come from the communities themselves. We can only encourage them to take action against these practices and support communities which do. In Janni for example,

A unit of barefoot doctors trained by Dr. Michaeli takes medical care to nomad families in the Eritrean lowlands. The unit includes a barefoot doctor, barefoot pharmacist and health information. **Below:** A dispensing pharmacist ensures the patient understands the dosage.

Left: The major thrust of the Eritrean Health Service is primary health care. When possible health care workers are trained to provide basic services within their own communities. *Below:* At a rural health center built by the local community from recycled materials, a woman peers shyly from a weekly prenatal care examination room.

The Eritrean Health Service produced a cheap, simple, "Third World" microscope: it costs $70 compared to $500 for a normal instrument. The World Health Organization refuses to endorse it because of Eritrea's political isolation.

people there have abolished all of these practices by common consent. Other places have not yet come so far but we expect it as they see the advantages of new ways of life. Women in particular have been affected. They have seen women in the EPLF existing on the same level as men. They see them doing every kind of work. They have helped to transport injured women fighters from the front. They have seen women medical staff treating them. These examples have made a big difference."

"For one reason or another," Dr. Nerayo continues, "people have come to believe that the medicines which we have and the medical workers (not all but most) are very effective. The competition between traditional medicine and the modern medicine groups has not happened in Eritrea. Eritrean society is being revolutionized by the struggle. Change is now more acceptable. Because of the war there has been a great interchange of cultures—people have seen different ways of doing things—sometimes improved ways—and even the most conservative are prepared to experiment with new ideas. One of these ideas is that there should be equality of men and women. One step in this direction is a scientif-

"It took a long time for us to build people's confidence in EPLF health services. This was especially true of the nomads. Slowly they understood that our medicine had something to offer and they had nothing to fear from us. Now they come here for care like this nomad girl who had breast cancer. I've just told her and her mother the operation was a success and she will recover. Building a health care system here will take decades."

ic understanding of biology and physiology. The National Union of Eritrean Women has taken significant steps in this direction; the creation of the sanitary napkin factory now provides better hygiene to 100,000 women but it is also part of a more general attempt to demystify menstruation—for women and men—one of the biological bases of discrimination against women. The same is true of the practice of clitorectomy and infibulation. Traditionally it is said this is done because the Koran demands it, which is not true, and also because the woman could be sexually active and lose her virginity and thus by sewing the labia together they prevent the male genitalia from entering her. But a woman can be sexually active even when infibulated and once it is understood that infibulation does not protect virginity nor is it demanded by the Koran, people will more easily give it up.

"Change is most effective when it comes from the people. We can only offer suggestions and examples; you cannot force people. You go around knocking on people's door for ten years to convince them to construct sanitary latrines and so on and you are not successful and then four or five influential people construct latrines—and you get latrines everywhere. It is the same with circumcision and infibulation; once the sentiment to stop it comes from the leadership of the community it will be stopped.

"In my experience it is not very difficult to change ideas about health. A simple example: eating cabbage.

Most people eat cabbage cooked but the main value of cabbage is as roughage. Beside that there is a small amount of vitamin C and minerals. If it is cooked you lose most of its food value; if it is eaten raw—especially if eaten daily for a week or so—it is very beneficial. So what we did, we cut the cabbage, added a little lemon juice and some oil: a salad. We tried it in the Orota hospital and three weeks later—300-400 kilometers away people started eating it like this!

"We had many people with bleeding gums. Once we explained there are wild leaves you can collect which when ground and mixed with oil can be eaten raw and are effective against bleeding gums. In four or five days all of the mountains were cleaned of these leaves—everyone was gathering and eating. And there wasn't a single case of bleeding gums. So that's why I say—people don't resist changes which can be demonstrated to be improvements. In general the Eritrean population is receptive to new ideas. That is why I think that once one sets proper priorities much can be achieved."

Dr. Assafaw, like most of the professionally trained Eritreans, could easily find a comfortable, well-paid position in the Middle East, Europe or North America. "Why am I here? I can't even answer that to myself. The experience of oppression makes us self-sacrificing. We have made substantial improvements in people's lives but what we really need is peace."

Amputated and blinded, this nomad shepherd boy recovers in the new civilian hospital—actually an operating room with outdoor post-operative care and a few tent wards. The director, Dr. Assafaw, sees daily the damage which the war and inadequate basic health care inflicts on the population. "This has gone on for 30 years: it is enough."

Bursting with pride, Amna, who once lived isolated, secluded, and uneducated, is now the head of a new poultry project in the Eritrean highlands. Each day she writes the date on the new eggs (something she could not have done two years ago) and distributes the eggs in the way the community decided; first to pregnant women, next to the sick and then to the old and young. Amna is being transformed by the changes taking place in Eritrea and she symbolizes its hopes for the future.

BIBLIOGRAPHY

Of particular interest are:

Burgess, Doris, Jenny Pearce, Jenny Rossiter, Trish Silkin. *Eritrean Journey*. London: War on Want, 1985.

Cliffe, Lionel and Basil Davidson, eds., *The Long Struggle of Eritrea for Independence and Constructive Peace*. Trenton: Red Sea Press, 1989.

"Conflict in the Horn of Africa," Special issue of the *Review of African Political Economy*, No. 30, September, 1984.

Davidson, Basil, Lionel Cliffe, and Bereket Habte Selassie, eds. *Behind the War in Eritrea*. London: Spokesman, 1980.

Eisenloeffel, Frits. *Famine in Eritrea*. Utrecht: Dutch Interchurch Aid, 1983.

Eisenloeffel, Frits and Inge Ronnback. *The Eritrean Durrah Odyssey*. Utrecht: Dutch Interchurch Aid, 1983.

Ethiopia and Eritrea. Woodford Green, Essex: Lalibela House, 1953.

Female Circumcision, Excision and Infibulation. Report No. 47. London: Minority Rights Group, revised edition 1985.

Fenet, Alain. *The Right of the Eritrean People to Self Determination*. Amiens, 1983.

Firebrace, James with Stuart Holland. *Never Kneel Down: Drought, Development and Liberation in Eritrea*. Trenton: Red Sea Press, 1984.

Gebre-Medhin, Jordan. *Peasants and Nationalism in Eritrea: A Critique of Ethiopian Studies*. Trenton: Red Sea Press, 1989.

Gilkes, Patrick. *The Dying Lyon: Feudalism and Modernisation in Ethiopia*. New York: St. Martin's Press, 1975.

Halliday, Fred and Maxine Molyneux. *The Ethiopian Revolution*. London: New Left Review, verso edition 1981.

Horn of Africa, Volume VI, No. 2, 1983. Special issue on Eritrea.

Human Rights Violations in Eritrea. Report of Amnesty International. London, 1978.

Journal of Eritrean Studies, Araia Tseggai, ed. Grambling State University, Post Box 894, Grambling, LA 71245 USA.

Kinnock, Glenys, and Jenny Matthews. *Eritrean Images of War and Peace*. London: Chatto and Windus, 1988.

Den Krieg in Eritrea beenden. Die Grünen in Bundestag (BRD). Documentation der Öffentlichen Anhörung zum Eritrea-Äthiopien Konflikt, 1986.

Lewis, I. M., ed. *Nationalism and Self Determination in the Horn of Africa*. London: Ithaca Press, 1983.

Machida, Robert. *Eritrea: The Struggle for Independence*. Trenton: Red Sea Press, 1987.

Pankhurst, E. S. *Eritrea on the Eve*. Woodford Green, Essex: New Times and Ethiopia News Books, 1952.

Petras, James. *The Eritrean Revolution and Contemporary World Politics*. Africa Research and Publications Project, Paper 2. Trenton, 1984.

Pool, David. *Eritrea: Africa's Longest War*. London: Anti-Slavery Society, 1980.

Selassie, Bereket Habte. *Conflict and Intervention in the Horn of Africa*. New York: Monthly Review Press, 1980.

———. *Eritrea and the United Nations and Other Essays*. Trenton: Red Sea Press, 1989.

Sherman, Richard. *Eritrea: The Unfinished Revolution*. New York: Praeger, 1980.

Trevaskis, G. K. N. *Eritrea: A Colony in Transition*. London: Oxford University Press, 1960.

Voice of Eritrean Women. Quarterly publication of the National Union of Eritrean Women. New York, Spring 1989.

War and Drought in Eritrea: A Collection of Clippings from Various English Language Newspapers and Magazines, 1984-85. Rome: Research and Information Centre on Eritrea (RICE), 1986.

Women in Eritrea. ERAC Educational Series, No. 4. Toronto: Eritrean Relief Association in Canada, n.d.

FURTHER INFORMATION

For further information, contact the following Eritrean Relief Association branches and affiliated committees:

AUSTRALIA
Eritrean Relief Committee
Pilgrim House
262 Pitt St., 4th floor
Sydney 2000
tel.: (02) 2646548
tlx.: 71 715 SYD ACC

BELGIUM
Comité Belge de Secours à
l'Erythrée
216 rue de Mérode
1060 Bruxelles
tel.: 02 539 3600
tlx.: 23743

ERA-CANADA
P.O. Box 2038
STN D Ottawa, Ontario
Canada K1P 5W3
tel.: (613) 234-2171
tlx.: 0636700435 MBX CA
fax: (613) 234-6213

DENMARK
Eritrean Relief Association
P.O. Box 2072
1013 Copenhagen
tel.: (01) 39 75 70/ 13 64 37

ERA FRANCE
Bereket Ghebretensae
5 rue Pierre Baundry
92140 Clanart

GERMANY
Eritrea-Hilfswerk in Deutschland
Hohenstaufenring 39
tel.: (0221) 23 84 38
tlx.: 8883297 ERA D
fax: (0221) 23 92 54

ITALY
Eritrean Relief Association Italy
Via Friuli 26
20135 Milano
tel.: (02) 54 68 223

ERA MIDDLE EAST
P.O. Box 20523
Safat, Kuwait

NETHERLANDS
Eritrean Relief Committee
Da Costastraat 88hs
1053 ZR Amsterdam
tel.: (020) 85 20 94

NORWAY
Den Eritreisk
Jhelporganisasjon i Norge
Karl Johans Gt-4
0458 Olso 4
tel.: (02) 38 58 72
tlx.: 79835 ERAN
fax: (02) 38 58 64

ERA SAUDI
c/o P.O. Box 5335
(Emanuel Kahsai)
Jeddah, Saudi Arabia

SWEDEN
Stodföreningen för Eritrea i
Sverige
Drottninggatan 16, 5tr
11151 Stockholm
tel.: (08) 10 91 97
tlx.: 19729 ERA-CON S

SWITZERLAND
Schweizerisches Unterstützungs-
komitee für Eritrea
Obere Gasse 26
5400 Baden
tel.: (056) 27 10 10/22 13 34

UNITED KINGDOM
Eritrea Relief Association
96 White Lion Street
London N1 9PF
tel.: (01) 837 9236
tlx.: 265871 MONREF G Quote
Ref. MM7316
fax: (01) 83 322 139

UNITED STATES
Eritrean Relief Committee
475 Riverside Drive, Suite 907
New York, NY 10115
tel.: (212) 870-2727
tlx.: 220310 NUES UR
fax: (212) 870-2736

Readers may also wish to contact: Research and Information Centre on Eritrea (RICE), Via della Dogana Vecchia 5, 10018 Rome, Italy.